# THE F

## IN MINUTES

# THE FUTURE
# IN MINUTES

KEITH MANSFIELD

Quercus

# Contents

# Introduction

You, the reader, are fortunate. In all of human history, now is the best time to be alive. Poverty is the lowest it has ever been; life expectancy the highest. Terrible diseases, such as smallpox and polio, have been eradicated. We can measure the pace of human progress since the agricultural revolution of ten thousand years ago, accelerating through later developments such as the Renaissance, the invention of printing, and the scientific and industrial revolutions. The dissemination of ideas and living in communities and then cities have driven this change. The invention of computers in the mid-20th century has now given each one of us almost all human knowledge at our fingertips; we're able to share ideas instantly with large networks of friends or colleagues – we've never been more connected.

Have we picked all of the ripe fruit of progress, meaning the gains will start to run out or even dissipate as society regresses? Does humanity even have a future? One difference from our past is that we've created the means to destroy ourselves. This is one of the daunting obstacles to overcome, but humans have demonstrated unparalleled ingenuity in this respect to date and if we look ahead and plan properly, there is every reason to believe we can advance far into a future filled with wonders. Consider this book an optimist's guide to that future, but one tinged with realism to allow that sunny outlook to bear fruit.

L.P. Hartley's *The Go-Between* opens with the line, 'The past is a foreign country; they do things differently there.' We must look to the future as our new homeland. This may seem difficult when the pace of change appears ever faster, when the trusted foundations that for most of our lives have anchored our homes and workplaces are found to have been made of sand, and as the great industrial monoliths of the past crumble, and entirely new unimagined entities rise from the rubble. But the future can be a welcoming place to those who embrace it, and better for humanity than any era that has gone before. In reading these pages I hope you will want to become a citizen of the future.

# The future begins now

Everything we see is past. Light takes time to reach our eyes, whether that's eight minutes from the Sun or just a nanosecond from the pages of this book. We cannot view the future the same way – it's invisible to us. But we need to acknowledge that the future is not some nebulous idea that begins twenty or one hundred years from now. Compared to when you began reading, you are already living in it.

We can view the past, but we cannot alter it. In contrast, the future is pure potential that humans can mould. Scientists map the four-dimensional canvas of space–time using light cones that show the areas of the future we are able to influence. We proceed there at a rate of one second per second. It's important not to become decoupled from the latest developments by 'future shock' – that we do not become daunted by the seemingly inexorable pace of progress. Recognizing that the future starts now will help us live successfully within it and take part in shaping its direction.

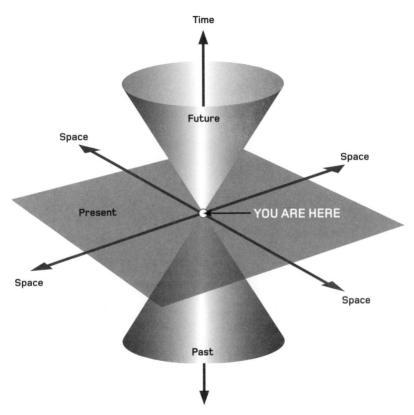

The four-dimensional canvas of space–time,
showing the future light cone humans can influence.

# Early visionaries

Predicting the future has come a long way since the Oracle at Delphi. In the 17th century, Robert Boyle listed 24 projects for science, including the likes of organ transplantation and permanent artificial lighting. In 1935, electronics pioneer Nikola Tesla wrote, 'In the twenty-first century the robot will take the place which slave labour occupied in ancient civilization.' Arthur C. Clarke foresaw the communications satellite in 1945 and the cell phone in 1976, while New York's World Fair of 1964 and its Progressland exhibit prompted an essay from Isaac Asimov looking fifty years ahead and anticipating driverless cars. But predicting the future isn't always so successful and many have missed the target. Clarke also anticipated bioengineering monkeys to provide a race of slave labour, while Asimov's essay expected cities spread across the ocean floor and on the Moon. One reason futurologists struggle to predict the future is that they fail to foresee disruptive changes that create a new technological landscape, such as the emergence of virtual humans (see page 292).

'The World of Tomorrow'. World's fairs
have always invited speculation on
the technology of the future.

# Utopias and dystopias

Man for all seasons, Sir Thomas More, published *Utopia* in 1516 (the title is a Greek pun sounding like both 'good place' and 'no place'). It depicts a supposedly idyllic fictional island republic that is antiwar, provides universal education and has no lawyers. But to show how views change over five hundred years, every household has two slaves, sex before marriage is punished by enslavement, euthanasia is encouraged and atheism thought immoral. In George Orwell's dystopian *Nineteen Eighty-Four* (written in 1948), mass surveillance means citizens do not know when their movements are being tracked or conversations listened to. Yet in the present most of the population embraces this happening through voluntarily acquired technology. For many of today's futurists, utopia looks similar to the civilization of Iain M. Banks's Culture novels in which humans and superintelligent 'minds' coexist and cooperate, hedonism fuelled by recreational drugs is rife and regular consciousness backups make people effectively immortal. If humanity exists millennia hence, all we can be certain of is that visions of utopia and dystopia will be very different still.

A woodcut of More's Island of Utopia, 1518.

# How we predict the future

To predict the future state of a system, scientists build a computer model and program how they believe its various elements interact. Initial conditions are input and this 'dynamic system' is run forwards through time. But weather forecasting exposes an unexpected effect of dynamic systems where the future cannot be accurately known. Some of the world's largest supercomputers are devoted to this, yet only look 7 to 10 days in advance – not due to their lack of processing power, but because of chaos theory's butterfly effect. Models are run many times in what are known as 'Monte Carlo simulations', a Bayesian statistics technique (see page 118) that forecasts different possible futures; a meteorologist then looks for similarities to see what's most likely. It's considerably easier to predict the climate in 15 years than the weather in 15 days. That's partly because long-term trends outweigh short-term effects, but much-longer-term predictions become harder again as they rely on anticipating future disruptions, such as brain uploading (see page 276) or The Singularity (see page 316).

# Why we predict the future

The axis of Stonehenge, in the United Kingdom, is perfectly aligned so that the Sun sets over it on the winter solstice, informing ancient forecasters of the shortest day. Knowing what is to come has helped humanity even before recorded history. Those early builders were mostly passive observers of the cycles of nature. Nowadays we forecast the future because we want to shape it. Buying extra of a material about to become scarce may help a corporation protect its supply chain or make more profit. Knowing the global temperature will rise by more than 2°C (3.6°F) by the end of the century unless we reduce carbon emissions is a good incentive to cut them. Predicting future population demographics may be another reason, but be wary. Given the Japanese population will become very elderly by the second half of this century, should the government encourage immigration or incentivize higher birthrates? Disruptive technology such as artificial intelligence (AI) might generate ample wealth to provide for the elderly, while a new generation of robots may be better equipped to care for them (see page 250).

# Age (in years)

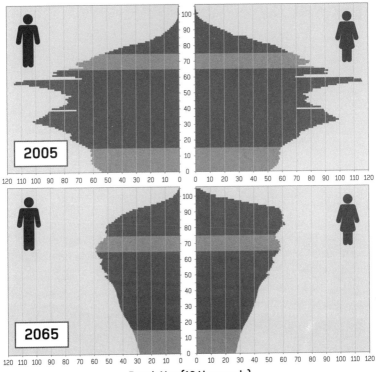

## Population (10 thousands)

Japanese population pyramid for 2005 and projection for 2065.

# Long-term thinking

Asked whether it is better to perform one action that saves a single life, or a second action that saves a billion humans, most people would think the latter is preferable. But what if the one life is in the present and the billion in the far future? There is a moral argument for thinking about the future in the same terms as the present.

In a paper entitled 'Astronomical waste: the opportunity cost of delayed technological development', Swedish philosopher Nick Bostrom argues that for every year that development of advanced technologies and the sustainable colonization of space is delayed, there is an extremely large price to pay in the value of good lives that would have been worth living, but whose potential has been snuffed out. Both the Effective Altruism movement and the 80,000 Hours organization have embraced this idea, believing that maximizing the overall human good throughout time should be the moral imperative of our age. Ensuring humanity has a long-term future is seen as pivotal to this endeavour.

The trolley bus dilemma: do we allow death and suffering in the present in exchange for trillions of additional better lives in the future?

# The pace of progress

Is the pace of progress increasing? By most measures, the answer is yes. Little materially would alter during an entire human lifetime until the Industrial Revolution. According to German economist Max Roser, since the effects began to be felt around 1800, infant mortality has fallen from 45% to below 5%. In the same period the percentage of people in extreme poverty has gone from 90% to under 10%. Just one lifetime ago, in 1945, global average life expectancy was 45 years – by 2018 it had reached 72. More people living closer together in cities made it easier to exchange ideas. Technology began the Industrial Revolution and new technologies have become synonymous with modern progress. Moore's law (see page 108), the doubling of computing power roughly every 18 months since the 1960s, is the engine of ever-quickening change. Looking ahead, many predict a coming technological 'Singularity' (see page 316) that will see a new step change, accelerating technology by many more orders of magnitude than the change wrought by the Industrial Revolution.

The Industrial Revolution heralded a step change in economic growth, bringing disruptive technologies such as the steam engine and the spinning jenny.

# Future shock

In their 1970 book *Future Shock*, Alvin and Heidi Toffler likened the rapid pace of change to the disorientating effects of culture shock. Unless we learn to control the rate of change, they believe we are doomed to a massive adaptational breakdown. In the posthumously published *The Salmon of Doubt*, Douglas Adams classified future shock in terms of age, noting that 'Anything that is in the world when you're born is normal and ordinary and is just a natural part of the way the world works.' The *Hitchhiker's Guide to the Galaxy* creator also highlights how difficult it is to adapt to new technologies when older, but identifies a sweet spot in which, if you are engaged with future ideas and technologies, then not only can they be exciting, but you can probably get a career in them.

Many people are working in jobs that didn't exist 20 or even 10 years ago. In a decade or two the same will still be true. The secret to countering future shock is to keep abreast of new developments, even as we age.

# The new futurists

Modern futurists have formed organizations expressly working towards ensuring that humanity has a future, and then trying to maximize overall long-term potential. Notable examples are the Future of Humanity Institute at Oxford, the Centre for the Study of Existential Risk at Cambridge, MIT's Future of Life Institute and the Machine Intelligence Research Institute based in Berkeley. Future-facing philanthropists help provide funding for these endeavours, either directly or through bodies such as San Francisco's Open Philanthropy Project.

In our lifetimes we expect to work for around 80,000 hours, hence the name of the 80,000 Hours organization (see page 18). This gives tailored advice to individuals in order to maximize the potential future good through their careers, such as working in AI safety research or becoming a 'China specialist' in their field. Citizens of the future have no mechanisms for repaying those in the present for undertaking this work; it is an act of selflessness unless we are considering our genetic descendants.

An annual AI developer conference hosted by Chinese AI company Baidu. The firm has joined Silicon Valley's Partnership for AI, allowing the possibility of future collaboration on AI safety.

# How we'll live

**G**iven that humans have seen centuries of astonishing progress, it's reasonable to hope that life in the future will be better than life in the early 21st century. To maintain momentum, in 2015 the United Nations adopted 17 Sustainable Development Goals (SDGs) for 2030. They include ending poverty and hunger, and ensuring good health, well-being and education, as well as protecting the planet. The goals are being monitored closely, with a 2018 report showing progress was not as rapid as needed to reach the ambitious target.

As we go further into the 21st century transformations are likely to be significant. Populations will rise, Earth will warm, lifespans will stretch and humans will live permanently in space. The biggest changes will be the ones we can't foresee – transformational inventions that completely disrupt the world as we know it. This is the definition of The Singularity (see page 316), the point at which artificial intelligence will change the way we live in ways our human intelligence is unable to comprehend.

# Family life

In richer nations over recent decades, fewer babies have been born, they've been born to older women, and the mothers have been less likely to be married. Children live at home for longer and grandparents play an increasing role in their development. There are more multi-family households and many adults now 'live apart together', enjoying a different balance of intimacy and autonomy. With same-sex marriage ever more accepted, households will continue to become more diverse.

In 2016, the first baby with three genetic parents was born in Mexico to Jordanian parents, helped by American scientists. The treatment removed a rare genetic disorder from the child's DNA, but why stop there? California already allows up to four parents on a birth certificate. With several parents involved, different genetic attributes could be chosen from each to produce 'designer' babies using gene-editing techniques (see page 248). For far future children, the concept of specific parents may seem very old-fashioned.

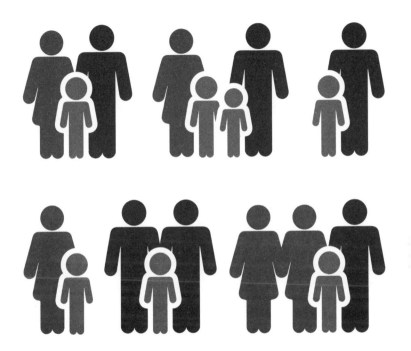

What is the future of the 'nuclear family'?

# Sex and marriage

Across the West, the onset of puberty has fallen from 11 to as young as 7 in girls in two decades. Reasons are complex but obesity is a factor. Despite this, teenagers are having less sex – in the United States sexual activity fell 14% for girls and 22% for boys between 1990 and 2015. Teenage pregnancy rates seemed out of control in the United Kingdom in the early 2000s, but numbers more than halved between 1998 and 2016 as an unexpected consequence of social media, with virtual interactions replacing physical ones – a trend mirrored elsewhere. Marriage rates may be falling, but reports of the institution's death have been exaggerated. In 2017, UK marriages averaged 12 years (the longest since 1972), divorce rates were at a 40-year low and a little over twice as many people got married as divorced. Same-sex marriages have strengthened the institution, the Netherlands allowing them in 2001, Britain (though not Northern Ireland) in 2014 and the United States in 2015. The trend towards liberalization continues with China likely to follow in the medium term. Yet even in 2018, homosexuality remained illegal in around 70 countries.

# Gender

Intersex babies have been born througout history, their gender not easily assigned as male or female. The nonassignment of a binary gender at birth has become a human rights issue with several international bodies calling for an end to clinical interventions on infants. In 2015 Malta became the first nation to outlaw nonconsensual modifications to sex characteristics. The 21st century has seen the rise of gender fluidity and a focus on transsexual rights. In 2018, the UK government still required a medical diagnosis of gender dysphoria (feeling your psychological identity to be different from your biological sex) in order to be legally recognized as other than your birth-assigned gender. Because few trans people applied, the idea of self-identifying without physical intervention was explored, but proved controversial among many in the feminist movement and remains unresolved. A post-gender future may be the natural consequence of a world in which same-sex relationships are no longer considered different to heterosexual relationships. In the future the controversy will be hard to understand.

# The future of work

The gig economy, a free-market system in which businesses contract workers for short-term engagements, was forecast by economist Ron Coase. Employees enjoy greater flexibility, while companies save on resources such as benefits, office space and training. Peer-to-peer transport company Uber is a classic example, and the future of work will see more instances of firms owning the infrastructure within which workers and consumers interact, while telepresence (see page 40) will bring more remote working. Technology promised more leisure time, but the working week in Europe continues to average 40 hours, with 47 hours in the US. Fears surrounding an AI-driven future include mass unemployment – the Royal Society states, 'current AI technologies are best suited to "routine" tasks, albeit tasks including complex processes, while humans are more likely to remain dominant in unpredictable environments, or in spheres that require significant social intelligence'. Another possibility is improving the work–life balance, with work defining us all less. Key will be how to share the benefits of the greater wealth created by the AI revolution.

The 40-hour working week was first adopted in the United States in 1940, with other countries following suit. Trade unions in the United Kingdom and Germany are actively campaigning for four-day weeks with full pay.

# Human-like robots

Osaka University's Hiroshi Ishiguro believes the tendency to anthropomorphize robots will see a desire for more androids in the future. It is a trend that has been seen in Hanson Robotics's human-like 'Sophia', modelled on movie star Audrey Hepburn. Sophia was debuted in 2016 and made a Champion of the UN Development Program the following year.

Though most future robots will look nothing like us, an obvious use for humanoid robots is sexual companionship (see page 64). Tactile robotic pets have been created for the elderly in Japan and more intense support may be offered by humanoids if the problems of the 'uncanny valley' can be overcome (see page 38). And while autopilots have been with us for a long time, Korean Pibot 2, released in 2016, is a physical humanoid autopilot with arms and legs to operate controls and the ability to liaise with air traffic control over the radio. The US Air Force is a fan, as it allows them to switch a human out of the cockpit without the need to modify their planes.

Hiroshi Ishiguro has created a double of himself called Geminoid to test theories of human–robot interaction.

# The uncanny valley

When French philosopher René Descartes lost daughter Francine to scarlet fever aged five, he is said to have constructed a lifelike clockwork replacement. In 1646, during an ocean voyage, sailors opened the casket containing the automaton, which sat up and spoke. In their revulsion they threw it overboard. This account foreshadows the 'uncanny valley' theory of Japanese roboticist Masahiro Mori, who hypothesized that our reaction to humanlike robots would shift from empathy to revulsion as they approach, but fail to reach, a lifelike human appearance. Only when a robot becomes indistinguishable from an organic human will we accept it. The implications are clear for future developers. Hollywood has a problem when animating life-like characters, with movies such as *The Polar Express* criticized for featuring a 'zombie train' populated by 'eerie' or 'creepy' characters. Perhaps the concept of mind–body dualism is at play here – that the two are separate, albeit interactive, entities – and only if, or when, artificial general intelligences become conscious (see page 330) will androids become accepted.

# Accepting human-like robots

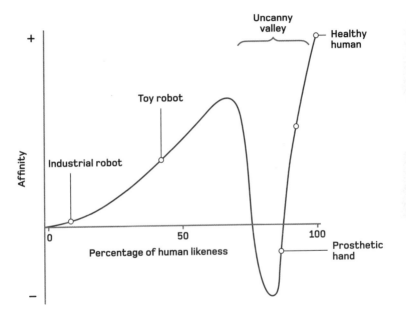

The 'uncanny valley', adapted from a graph devised by Masahiro Mori, with affinity on the vertical axis versus human likeness along the horiontal.

# Telepresence

Telepresence is being in a location, without actually being there. AI pioneer Marvin Minsky coined the term with Patrick Gunkel in 1980, likening it to teleportation (see page 380) by experiencing sensory input from a distant location. Having a physical avatar in another place allows richer interactions, and telepresence robots serve in a range of corporate, manufacturing and educational environments. In 2017, the American Natural History Museum and French Musée de la Grande Guerre each began experimenting with telepresence for those physically incapable of visiting with others. In the future, we'll spend physical time each day with distant elderly relatives, the robot working as an assistant when not 'possessed' by a human. More advanced telepresence will allow users to affect the distant environment using robotic arms and haptic feedback. Further ahead, it could become increasingly tailored to individuals in the form of personal avatars. And through this technology, if we ourselves think the journey is unnecessarily dangerous or expensive, it would provide a means of 'beaming up' to a future moonbase (see page 344).

Currently in development at Suitable Technologies, the BeamPro2 telepresence robot could help facilitate specialist consultations and patient visits irrespective of location.

# Mass unemployment

In the 19th century, 'Luddites' destroyed the new-fangled weaving machinery of the Industrial Revolution to protest at loss of employment or lowering of wages. The future will see similar resistance to change through technological progress.

A 2017 McKinsey Global Institute report forecasts 375 million jobs (and possibly up to 800 million) will be lost worldwide to automation through AI by 2030. The greater effects will happen in developed economies due to higher wages incentivizing automation. Forbes forecasts taxi drivers will start being replaced in the early 2020s with an end to most human freight drivers by 2025. All workers will need to adapt through additional education and to focus on activities that require greater social and emotional skills, creativity or high-level cognitive capabilities. The forecasts accept automation will also create jobs that do not yet exist, but given the dramatic changes, it will be imperative for governments to develop mechanisms that support workers through changing times.

# Universal basic income

According to economist Robin Hanson, our era is a 'dream time' – a blip in the history of humanity in which working humans are well paid. Until the Industrial Revolution, more than 80% of the world's population existed on subsistence wages. Many economists argue that our future economy, driven by automation, will see a return to ultra-low wages – even though far more overall wealth will be generated globally by an army of robot workers guided by AI.

If governments can continue to tax the profits, it is proposed they keep citizens out of poverty by providing a universal basic income, a flat payment to everyone irrespective of need. If this sounds far-fetched, the Swiss held a referendum in 2016 to see if they should adopt this. While the proposal was only supported by 23% of voters, trials in Madhya Pradesh (India), Quatingha Velho (Brazil) and Rarieda (Kenya) have shown many benefits, such as specifically empowering women by lifting them out of poverty. As we progress further into this century, nations appear likely to adopt the idea.

On 4th October 2013, Swiss campaigners for a universal basic income dumped eight million five-cent coins (one per inhabitant) in Bern's Bundesplatz, to celebrate collecting more than 125,000 signatures to instigate a referendum.

# Cryptocurrencies

In 2008 'Satoshi Nakamoto', whose identity remains unknown, devised Bitcoin, an encrypted digital currency independent of government. The system solved the problem of spending the same bitcoins more than once by creating a distributed open-source ledger, the blockchain (see page 86), and rewarding users for devoting the computer resources necessary to verify transactions – a process termed 'mining'. The total number of bitcoins is limited mathematically – scarcity helping maintain value.

Bitcoin became a blueprint for other cryptocurrencies. The Ethereum blockchain (launched 2015) is a way of recording unbreakable smart contracts. It allows companies to raise capital through Ethereum-based tokens rather than by borrowing from banks, so making the tech revolution a self-sustaining ecosystem. Other developments include the cryptocurrency Iota, designed for transactions between devices on the Internet of things (see page 80). Even mega corporations such as Amazon and Alphabet are speculated to be considering cryptocurrencies of their own.

# Synthetic meat

Maintaining livestock uses 30% of Earth's land surface and 8% of its water, and is responsible for 18% of greenhouse gas emissions. As people become richer, their cravings for meat increase. By 2050 it's anticipated that demand will be more than double that at the beginning of the 21st century. While this sounds like a recipe for disaster, it may be that another dish will save the planet. In 2013 MosaMeat's first lab-grown burger, cultivated from cow cells and priced at $330k, was eaten in London. Costs are plummeting with a projected price of $10 by 2022.

Silicon Valley's Impossible Foods had burgers for under $20 available across America and parts of Asia. They claim their plant-based burger looks, feels, tastes, smells and even bleeds like real meat, using a soy-derived, lab-grown compound called heme. However it happens, the future must see a shift to synthetic meat to satisfy a growing population's carnivorous appetite while preserving the planet – which will look very different when there's no longer the need for domesticated livestock.

The plant–based ingredients of Impossible Foods' 'burger meat'.

# Innovative food sources

Two billion people actively consume insects as part of their diet. In 2013, the United Nations released a report entitled 'Edible insects: Major prospects for food and feed security', arguing insects can offer an environmentally friendly, nutritious solution for feeding the world by 2050. An intermediate step will be turning them into high-protein animal feed – crickets use just $\frac{1}{12}$ of the resources of a cow to produce the same amount of protein. Among those who practise 'entomophagy', beetles and caterpillars top the menu, along with bees, wasps and ants. The downside is that 5.5 billion people are disgusted by the prospect, so innovative ways of making insects palatable will be required.

Algaculture is another potential source of protein, particularly as it doesn't need fresh water. Spirulina, derived from blue-green algae, produces seven times as much protein as soy beans using the same amount of land. Florida horticulturalist Mark Settles began experiments on the International Space Station in 2018 to investigate the future possibility of farming algae in space.

NASA's Space Algae
investigation on the ISS.

# Drink and drugs

Although currently on the rise in China, alcohol consumption is falling across all ages in the West (most dramatically among the young), with a major drop in drinking out only partially offset by drinking more at home. However, in 2015, former British government drugs advisor and neuropsychopharmacologist David Nutt created alcosynth, a nontoxic inebriant that mimics the effects of alcohol without hangovers, toxicity, aggression or loss of control. Society is likely to shift towards such designer-drug substitutes, perhaps even leading to David Hughes's paradise engineering (see page 72) in coming centuries.

The UN forecasts a 25% rise in illegal drug use by 2050. In 2018, Canada joined several American states in legalizing cannabis, but it may take clear results from this decision before other nations follow. Also, as we receive ever more of our sensory input digitally, culminating in neural interfaces, software will be able to tailor our states of perception, giving rise to a new era of digital drugs.

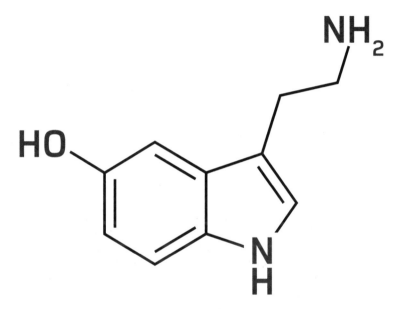

The chemical structure of neurotransmitter serotonin, sometimes known as the 'happy chemical'. Ecstasy and LSD significantly raise serotonin levels.

# Mixed reality

Mixed, or augmented, reality enhances the real world, placing additional transparent layers over our existing senses. You can already play mixed-reality games, such as *Pokémon Go*; soon face recognition will allow you to greet a stranger as a long-lost friend and your spirit animal to guide you through a new city. As the Internet of things (see page 80) spreads, new and innovative ways of assimilating data using mixed-reality overlays and interfaces that understand user context will be required. Just as mixed-reality apps have introduced virtual pets to the home, people will also store digital versions of their living pets so that, when gone, they can be resurrected in mixed reality. They will still take a beloved dog for a walk or stroke a long-dead cat with haptic feedback. Why stop there? Dead friends and relatives could be brought back to life in this mixed-reality world. Initially only one person will see these ghosts, but with Google's proposed Cloud Anchor technology, which will enable shared mixed-reality experiences, the virtual and the real will merge.

Destination 249 m

# Invisibles

We call it a mobile or cell 'phone', but this device is so successful because it's also a camera, music player, TV screen, GPS, health tracker, eReader and very much more. We don't want to be encumbered by multiple devices, preferring to travel light. The early 21st century saw manufacturers pushing additional gadgets such as the Apple watch, Fitbit trackers and myriad health sensors, with little enthusiasm from the public. These 'wearables' will prove a transitory phase until the additional gizmos instead become 'invisibles', much more seamlessly integrated with our bodies.

In 2014, Google proposed a smart contact lens to monitor blood-sugar levels in tears for diabetes. In 2015, Magic Leap's Eric Tremblay demonstrated a contact lens to help with macular degeneration that zoomed on blinking. And as cochlear implants improve to superhuman hearing levels, people will also have them implanted to stream music or receive remote audio information.

An artist's conception of smart lens technology.

# Fashion

Fashion is a means of self-expression. It's about art, culture and, increasingly, science. For example, Japanese fashion entrepreneur Yusaku Maezawa's 'Zozosuit' captures your personal measurements at home each time you want to shop for made-to-measure Zozo clothes online. He hopes to use the technology for spacesuits on a 2023 'dear Moon' lunar mission with SpaceX. In the West, clothes have become cheaper and more disposable through the use of low-cost labour elsewhere in the world, but this is unsustainable in its wastefulness of resources, and sometimes unethical. In the future, disposable clothes worn as one-offs will figure prominently through 3D printing. In 2017, designer Danit Peleg created an entire 3D-printable collection using desktop printers from home. She is currently working on making files available for open-source download and purchase, which will allow customers to print a garment directly at home or at designated printing stores. When they tire of it, they simply reuse the material to create a new design. Such a process will lead to the democratization of fashion, where everyone can create and license new designs.

Danit Peleg's Imagine Jacket, the world's first ready-to-wear, 3D-printed garment available to buy online.

# Shopping and retail

A mazon and China's Alibaba are among the world's most valuable companies. Besides functioning as conventional online retailers, both enable a 'marketplace' through which other sellers can reach a vast public, in exchange for a percentage of sales. Their success confirms an ongoing trend that sees online retail rapidly increasing its share of the global market.

Offline, businesses have tried to hold the line by improving the shopping experience – stores as social spaces as well as being physical windows on a more comprehensive online presence. The arrival of mixed reality (see page 54) has allowed customers to see how a new sofa would look in their living room or to try on clothes via an augmented mirror. Understanding your customers will be the biggest secret of future retail, whether on- or offline, all made possible through the big data we share (see page 110). Further ahead, nanotechnology will bring radical abundance (see page 372), making 'buying things' obsolete.

Clearance sale: to survive online competition, offline businesses must adapt by knowing their customers and offering them richer experiences.

# Sport

In 2018, Kenyan Eliud Kipchoge ran the Berlin marathon in 2:01:39. Once thought impossible, the two-hour barrier will fall in the 2020s, but the trend in ever-better performance is waning. Italian clinical biochemist Giuseppe Lippi claims men have reached 99% of their natural physiological limit, with women catching up fast. Increasing future limits to athletic performance will be determined less and less by the innate physiology of the athlete, and more and more by scientific and technological advances, raising the question of where to draw the line between what is 'natural' and what is artificially enhanced. Sport will change as competitors experiment with augmentation, becoming society's testing ground for new technologies. A safety-first approach in many sports will result in developments such as the banning of heading in soccer, and will lead to a rise in eSports – multiplayer videogame contests in spectator arenas. And once humans live in space, the sporting landscape will change further – first seen with Alan Shepard's 1971 lunar golf strike, which travelled over a mile.

A multiplayer esport event in Moscow, in which teams of five compete against each other playing the *Dota 2* videogame.

# Robot sex

Sex drives much innovation, and in the robot revolution sexbots are one of the technologies furthering human-like physical and emotional interactions. In 2018, RealBotix™ unveiled 'Harmony' (with a £15,000 price tag), claiming it to be a lifelike female humanoid robot with AI, a Scottish accent and the anatomical capability to have sex. 'Henry' followed soon after. Both offer the opportunity to fulfil an obvious need regarding loneliness or difficulty in forming relationships.

Sergi Santos of sex robot company Synthea Amatus hopes the rise of sex robots will curb prostitution and sex trafficking, and this is something for policy makers to consider, but the topic remains controversial. Robot ethicist Kathleen Richardson founded the Campaign Against Sex Robots in 2015, believing that the female versions objectify women. Houston City Council has altered local statutes in a way that prevented Toronto firm KinkySDollS opening a sex robot brothel. Despite such legal blocks, history tells us it is unlikely to prevent developments in this area.

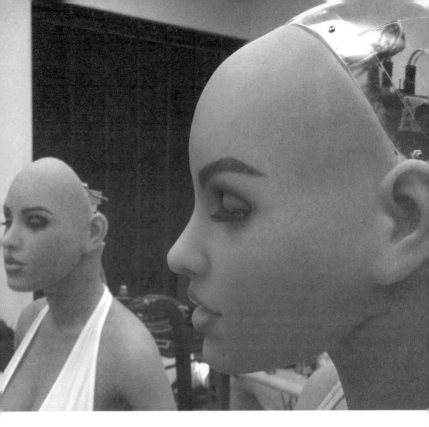

Harmony, from RealBotix™.

# Entertainment

The increasing popularity of streaming services suggests scheduled broadcast TV will disappear with the current generation, except for 'events'. Even there, innovation is required, evidenced by Telemundo Deportes and the BBC's virtual reality (VR) coverage of the football World Cup. This is part of a shift in entertainment that sees the viewer increasingly central to the overall experience. It will be further demonstrated in the continued rise of videogames, driven by both cell phones and the hyperrealistic experiences of more immersive platforms. Players already number more than one-third of the world's population, nearly half female. Virtual performers will also replace humans, exemplified by Abba's 2020 tour by representations of their 1979 selves and deceased film stars continuing to make movies. All this content highlights the importance of personalized algorithmic recommendation systems in both visual and musical entertainment, with consumers less willing to risk investing time without guarantees of a rewarding experience.

Abba performing in 1979.

# Gamification

Gamification employs game-design elements to improve user engagement, organizational productivity, HR issues and more. Between 2009 and 2011, Farmville helped Facebook grow from 200 million to 750 million active users, attracting the older generation to social media for the first time. In 2018, comedian Samantha Bee created the trivia game app 'This is not a game' to persuade young people to register to vote in the US midterm elections. In his book *The Gamification Revolution* (2013), Canadian Gabe Zichermann argued it allowed companies to create unprecedented levels of user engagement with customers and employees. David Chandross of Toronto's Baycrest Health Sciences says the principal shift will be the construction of '3-D, immersive locations that players can explore' and cites health and education as prime application areas. He argues that this future will see the creation of virtual spaces where people's progress is tracked by medics or educators or their AI counterparts and says, 'you will live in two worlds, the real one, and a virtual one which archives your data for professional or personal use.'

In the fitness app Zombies Run, the user sprints for their life to escape zombies.

# Personalized education

A single teacher disseminating the same material to a relatively large group of students will soon end. In the future we'll learn at our own pace following our own interests, receiving individually tailored education devised and delivered by artificial intelligence. The Gates Foundation is one of many investors in personalized education, helping develop a range of digital tools to deliver lessons and assess performance so that teachers can dedicate more time to helping those who struggle.

Brighter humans will benefit, too. Future education won't stop on leaving school or university. Lifelong learning is essential for reskilling or self-improving in a future when most work is performed by machines. Massive open online courses (MOOCs) have allowed students to study with many of the world's top institutions. The promise is immense: that one million people a year could study the Cambridge mathematics tripos or take an MBA at the Harvard Business School.

MIT, IBM and Harvard are among the many institutions offering MOOC courses on a range of computer sciences.

# Paradise engineering

Many transhumanists (see page 278) think one of the future drivers of our existence will be fun. In his 1995 book *The Hedonistic Imperative*, philosopher David Pearce outlines how designer drugs, genetic engineering and nanotechnology (see page 372) could be used to replace suffering with 'gradients of bliss'. He predicts that moments of peak happiness today will be insignificant to the hedonistic highs to come, which will form a 'bedrock of invincible mental health'.

Critics of Pearce's hedonistic utilitarianism argue that it values bliss over so-called called higher ideals such as self-realization, education, love or wisdom, and that the focus on minimizing suffering is too one-dimensional. They suggest that our response to suffering is one of the things that makes us human.

Pearce remains adamant that the best potential future for humans, and other animals that we can help experience it, is one of unbridled pleasure.

David Pearce proposes that by the year 3000 we will be in a position to reengineer the basis of all life on Earth to create paradise across the planet.

# Universal translators

In 2010, Word Lens was released – holding a phone's camera over a piece of text in one language saw it translated into another, without an online connection. When Google created smart glasses, Word Lens enabled wearers to see any text in their own language. As of 2018 Skype offered instantaneous translation in 10 languages, with a further 50 available for texting. Google's Pixel earbuds can translate 40 languages in real time. Machine learning is very effective in this area and it's claimed that automatic translators will soon take more than half the $40 billion annual translation market. With this technology, language learning is likely to become niche. Once human languages have been mastered, the technology may be applied to animals, a view espoused by Con Slobodchikoff in his book *Chasing Dr Dolittle*, and something that would have profound implications for animal rights (see page 196). Amazon anticipates rudimentary pet translators in the 2030s and, if we can talk to the animals, it might even become possible to talk with the aliens when we make first contact.

BIENVENIDO
AL FUTURO
Spanish to English
WELCOME
TO THE FUTURE

# Evolution of language

Evolutionary biologist Mark Pagel argues that language is social technology for enhancing cooperation. The two most widely spoken are Mandarin Chinese and English, and the two most successful nations are China and the United States. English is more accessible to most, owing to its restricted character set and widespread second-language use. Every year, 30 to 50 of the world's 8,000 languages die out. Pagel wonders if the future of language is for us to be 'one world speaking one language' in which case it would be English. Emojis are an example of new language emerging. Another happened in 2017, when a Facebook bot experiment to achieve better communication with humans was stopped because the bots began communicating with each other in nonstandard ways. In computing, we use high-level languages resembling human language in preference to strictly numerical machine code. But there's no obvious reason for computers to communicate in English once they become more intelligent than humans, so the future of language is how machines will use it.

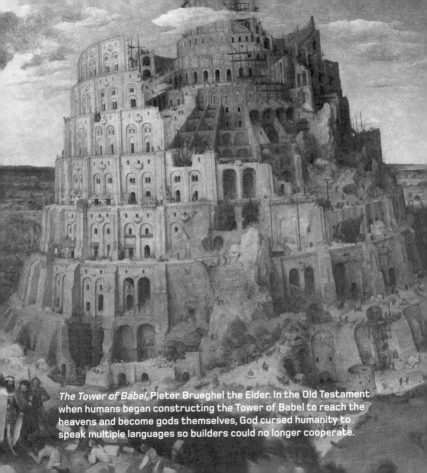

*The Tower of Babel*, Pieter Brueghel the Elder. In the Old Testament when humans began constructing the Tower of Babel to reach the heavens and become gods themselves, God cursed humanity to speak multiple languages so builders could no longer cooperate.

# Building the future

A technological future requires both a visible and an invisible backbone. In 1858, the first transatlantic cable was laid, cutting communication time between Europe and North America from several days to a few minutes. Nowadays nearly a thousand communications satellites connect the world at the speed of light, with space-based Internet from companies such as SpaceX following fast behind. On Earth, our hunger for energy will require superconducting transmission lines. The need for wireless bandwidth will mean masts built into every structure. With more humans living in larger cities, sewage plants will be transformed, using revolutionary bacteria, into highly profitable factories for clean water, energy, plastics and fertilizers. With 71% of Earth's surface covered by water, there'll be expansion on and below oceans. Ultimately, physical infrastructure, limited by the constraints of materials and physical laws, will give way to digital forms. Great future architectural projects are more likely to happen in a virtual world, but to the citizens of the future, that won't make them any less real.

An artist's conception of sustainable domes and power grids.

# The Internet of things

In 1991, Xerox PARC's Mark Weiser wrote, 'The most profound technologies are those that disappear. They weave themselves into the fabric of everyday life until they are indistinguishable from it.' He was talking about the Internet of things – the transition from computers being standalone devices to becoming embedded

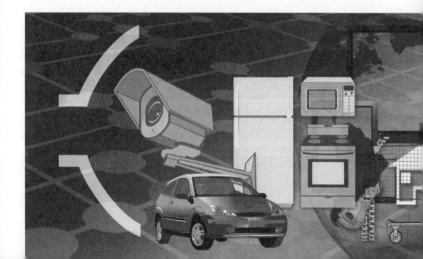

into most industrial and household items. Early ideas were monitoring liquid levels in the work canteen coffeepot and having vending machines reorder low-running stock. Advances in the Web, miniaturization and sensors mean that growth is moving apace. Privacy and security become issues — when your cutlery can analyze your food for you, might the information be sent to your doctor and even your health-insurance company? The volume of sensory data generated requires new and novel ways of interacting with it, beyond simply swiping a screen. To capitalize, humans will need new built-in interfaces.

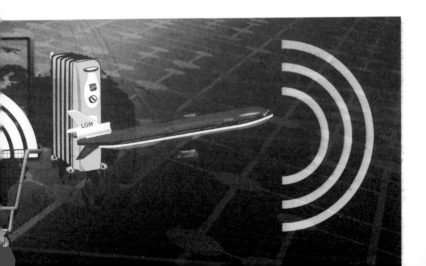

# Additive manufacturing

While conventional printing adds a layer of ink onto a sheet of paper, 'additive manufacturing' builds a three-dimensional object, layer by layer, using different materials. Better known as 3D printing, the technology was conceived in the 1980s but heavily patented. As patents expire, various possibilities are emerging. Low-cost fused filament fabrication involves extruding molten material from a moving print nozzle into the desired shape. It is already used for rapid prototyping. Selective laser sintering uses a laser beam to solidify areas of each two-dimensional layer as a shape is built – components of the F-18 fighter are made in this way. A single device producing anything from body parts to rocket engines is like a sci-fi replicator, but operates more slowly. The International Space Station has such a gadget and it will become a staple of all future space missions – utilizing onboard design databases or templates transmitted by Earth-based engineers. But technology can be used for bad. Designs already exist for 3D-printed guns, signalling the likelihood that such weaponry will be downloaded and printed in the future.

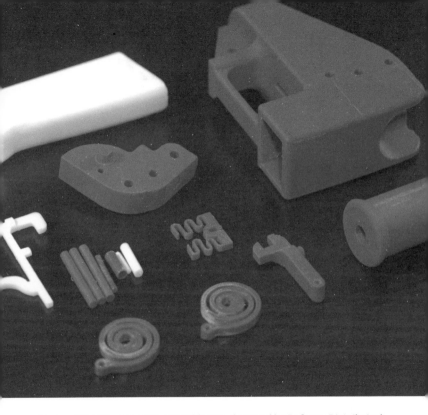

Parts of the Liberator 3D-printable gun, designed by Defense Distributed and currently banned in the United States.

# Virtual reality

Electronic signals in our brains create the impression of a real external world; virtual reality (VR) is the closest technology we have to simulating this process. Already used in education to interact with dinosaurs or visit other planets, VR technology is also becoming vital in cutting-edge industries. It is used by America's Cup and Formula One teams to trial technologies, and space projects use VR to make the brain believe it is in a low-gravity environment. Games and immersive entertainment will be the biggest short-term future driver, even fully sharing 'celebrity' experiences. Mainstream acceptance will likely only happen if the current hardware constraints of VR goggles and headphones disappear, as with special effects company Framestore's school field trip that takes schoolchildren on a bus ride across Mars. The ultimate endpoint is direct stimulation to the sensory areas of the brain. If the pace of technological progress continues, it is inevitable that VR will reach the point where it is indistinguishable from reality – unless we are already there.

Framestore's 'Field Trip to Mars': students marvel at the Martian landscape visible from the windows of their yellow schoolbus.

# Blockchain

In 2008, one 'Satoshi Nakamoto' invented the blockchain to support the first cryptocurrency, Bitcoin (see page 46). While Satoshi's true identity remains unknown, blockchain has emerged as a key future technology. It's an open, distributed ledger that records transactions between two parties in an efficient, verifiable and permanent way. A growing chain of linked blocks is protected by a cryptographic 'hash' – verified by 'miners' – that encodes information using a mathematical construct called a Merkle tree. Hackers would need quantum computers (see page 120) or to gain control of more than 50% of the entire ledger (considered impossible due to its scale and widespread location) to overcome the security. Blockchains will be useful in smart contracts (verifiable electronic agreements) and all manner of financial deals. Efforts are underway to create land registry blockchains with future applications expected to be voter verification in elections, handling medical data and giving individuals control of their digital identities through their biometric information, without recourse to stored passwords or centralized databases.

# How the Blockchain Works

**Transaction A**  **Transaction B**  **Transaction C**  **Transaction D**

⬇  ⬇  ⬇  ⬇

| Hash value #A | Hash value #B | Hash value #C | Hash value #D |

**Transaction X; data of any length**

⬇

Hash value #X

Unique value of fixed length

Hash value #AB    **MERKLE TREE**    Hash value #CD

Combined hash value #ABCD

Hash of Block 49

Timestamp

Nonce

**Block 48**  **Block 49**  **Block 50**

Individual data are converted into hashes that are then combined through a Merkel tree. Once miners calculate the nonce, a mathematical 'proof of work', the new block can be added to the chain.

# Urbanization

In 2018, 55% of the world's population was urban, with the United Nations predicting a rise to 68% by 2050 – by which time the rural population is projected to decline by 300 million. City dwellers numbered only 751 million in 1950, but by 2018 it was 4.2 billion. At the time, Tokyo was the greatest of 33 megacities with 37 million inhabitants, followed by New Delhi with 29 million. While Asia has more megacities, the Americas are the most urbanized region. By 2030 there will be 10 more megacities, mostly in developing countries, influx from rural areas and birthrate contributing equally. Urban living is linked with higher levels of literacy and education, better health, lower fertility but higher life expectancy, greater access to services and enhanced opportunities for cultural participation. Downsides include congestion and increasing air pollution that electric vehicles and tunnelling (see page 96) will help address. Greater connectivity has been the biggest driver of urbanization, but with future humans connecting virtually rather than physically, the benefits listed above will continue to be the dominant pulling factors.

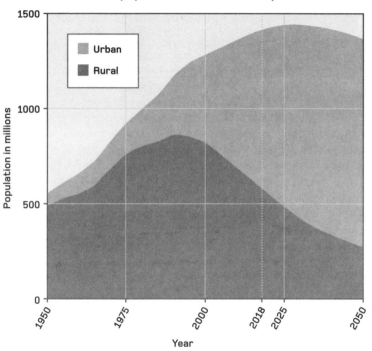

## The variation of China's urban and rural populations over a century

**Legend:**
- Urban
- Rural

Year

Population in millions

By 2050, the UN Population Division forecasts four-fifths
of the Chinese population will live in urban areas.

# Smart cities

Will Wright's 1989 video game sensation *Sim City* proved inspirational for both urban planners and computer geeks, creating the vision for smart cities in which technology oversees traffic and transportation systems, power plants, water supplies, waste management, law enforcement, schools, libraries, hospitals and other services. The Internet of things (see page 80) will make this possible. An early example came in 2011 with the app Smart Bump. As Boston's citizens drove, accelerometers in their cell phones detected potholes, the app sending their locations to City Hall. Even if artificial intelligences manage cities in the future, we must be mindful their algorithms will still reflect political choices. Future humans must also be smart in deciding how to balance priorities before computers implement them. The smarter cities become, the more secure their digital infrastructure needs to be, especially as we proceed to automated, self-sustaining cities where robotic workers sweep the streets, deliver goods and build infrastructure by anticipating future trends.

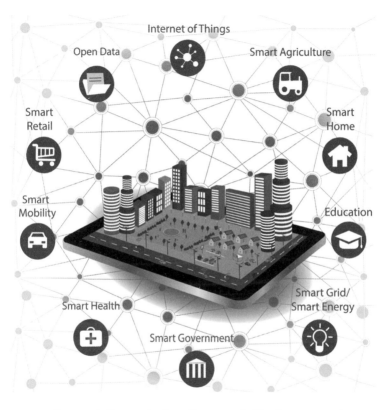

The smart city: eventually we'll see smart cities become smart
countries and then a fully connected and integrated smart world.

# Floating cities

With living space at a premium as populations rise through the 21st century (see page 88), urban centres in coastal areas or with waterways can either reclaim land (as with Hong Kong International Airport) or use the marine environment for floating houseboats, offices, hospitals or prison ships. To supplement growing cities the Smart Floating Farm project envisages modular, three-tiered structures topped with solar panels, a middle level for hydroponics to grow crops and, beneath the water, an area for aquaculture farming fish and other marine animals. The proof-of-concept Floating Island Project in French Polynesia looks further ahead to bespoke 'seasteads' providing accommodation and a special economic seazone with a considerable degree of autonomy. The end goal sees floating habitats beyond territorial waters allowing for new political structures. Ultimately, cities don't have to float on water. The speculative Clouds Architecture Office in New York envisages nomadic 'cloud skippers', autonomous communities circumnavigating the globe.

An artist's conception of a floating Prismatic Island

# Building up

As urbanization increases, one way to accommodate rising populations is to build higher. The accolade of world's tallest building has always been prized and the 2020s will see the first kilometre structures, led by the Jeddah Tower in Saudi Arabia. The higher the floor, the bigger the premium tenants will pay; as materials and techniques develop, ambition will see mile-high towers. But there are plans to transform the future urban landscape more radically. Canadian firm Thoth Technologies has patented a 20km (12.5 mile) inflatable tower that would double as a space launch platform, significantly reducing the amount of fuel required to reach low-Earth orbit. But why build up when it's less of an engineering challenge to hang downward from supports? Clouds Architecture Office has proposed the supertall Analemma Tower, suspended from an orbiting asteroid. Powered by solar energy with the upper structures benefiting from uninterrupted sunlight, and extracting water from passing clouds, the 32km (20 mile) main structure would follow a daily figure-of-eight pattern between the northern and southern hemispheres.

ThothX inflatable tower and
space launch platform with an
external elevator cabin (lower)

THOTHX TOWER

# Tunnelling

Cities are three-dimensional spaces. A limiting factor to a well-functioning urban environment is that transport operates primarily in two dimensions at ground level. Opened in 1863, London's underground railway was the first attempt to make transport 3D. Many major cities followed suit, yet above ground congested urban highways continue to divide communities. Boston's 'Big Dig', completed in 2007, tried to rectify this, but huge cost overruns demonstrated the difficulties and expense of tunnelling. Heading downwards will only be possible if tunnelling costs can be reduced by orders of magnitude. To drive such innovation, Elon Musk has founded The Boring Company, its vision involving ever-expanding tunnels with unlimited numbers of levels to enable high-speed transit to any destination – a prototype tunnel opened in 2018. Eventually taking all utilities underground and out of view will lead to beautiful urban spaces free from vehicles and transmission lines, with tunnels being extended across continents when looking further ahead.

As part of its research, The Boring Company built a test tunnel in Hawthorne, California.

# Hyperloops

In 1964, the 250kmh (155mph) Japanese Shinkansen or 'bullet train' began a new era of high-speed rail. When, in 2012, a high-speed rail connection between San Francisco and Los Angeles was approved, with the initial phase due between 2027 and 2033, Elon Musk expressed disappointment at the pedestrian pace. Instead he proposed a radical new technology – a 'hyperloop' – that could cut the intended 160-minute journey time to under half an hour, with speeds up to 1,200kmh (745mph). A capsule, or pod, travels in a low-pressure tunnel, with an electric fan mounted on the front to transfer high-pressure air to the rear. It could be built on pylons alongside existing highways with solar panels providing power, though in the future tunnels would take the system underground. Richard Branson's Virgin Hyperloop One has since signed agreements with several governments to develop hyperloops over coming decades. Further ahead, hyperloops are ideal for low-pressure environments such as the surfaces of the Moon or Mars – at least until Mars is terraformed (see page 348).

Virgin Hyperloop One.

# Autonomous transportation

The first aircraft autopilot was developed by Sperry Corporation in 1912; London Underground's Victoria Line began automatic train operation in 1967; modern airliners and spacecraft largely fly themselves. Autonomous cars will improve traffic flow and provide enhanced mobility for the elderly and disabled. They will save millions of lives and, powered by electricity, reduce greenhouse gas emissions. Through car-sharing, they'll relieve congestion and pressure on parking. However, the Center for Global Policy Studies forecasts up to four million American truck-, bus-, delivery- and taxi-driving jobs lost if the move happens quickly. The gig economy has seen a dramatic, but short-lived, rise in human delivery until self-driving and drones become the norm. A less obvious consequence will be a dramatic decline in organs for transplantation, given far fewer road-traffic fatalities. And how should self-driving cars handle unavoidable accidents? If schoolchildren are crossing a road and the only way to avoid them is to drive over a cliff, would you want your vehicle taking the autonomous decision to kill you?

The EDIT self-driving car.

# Drones

The military has been at the forefront of unmanned aerial vehicles, or drones, for decades. Successful at reconnaissance in the 1990s war in the former Yugoslavia, the *Predator* became armed early this century; smaller, hand-launched portable attack drones such as *Switchblade* are popular in tactical situations. Amazon Air and Google Wing are major drone delivery programmes – the biggest likely growth area in the immediate future – but it was Matternet who became the first company to be licensed to fly over dense urban environments. Numbers look set to escalate with other uses including infrastructure and building inspections and for police and fire departments.

Entirely autonomous drones will be in use in the near future and, by 2030, ground-based lasers will recharge drones allowing them to remain airborne permanently. Civilian drones will vary in scale from people carriers down to insect-sized flying machines with enormous implications for privacy.

With its first successful delivery trial in 2017, Matternet has also pioneered the use of drones for delivering medical supplies to disaster areas.

# Flying cars

Flying cars already exist, but are a far cry from the images of science fiction. The first 'limousine of the air' was unveiled as early as 1917, at New York's American Aero Expo; sadly the Curtiss Autoplane only hopped. Slovakia's 2014 Aeromobil is authentic, reaching 160kmh (100mph), wings folded back on the highway, and 360kmh (220mph) when airborne. It has a transition time of only a few minutes between configurations, but needs a runway for takeoff and landing and a pilot's licence to fly. The 'flying car' of the near future will be a drone such as the Chinese Ehang 184 quadcopter taxi, which carries two passengers up to 10km (6 miles). New Zealand in partnership with Google founder Larry Page's Kitty Hawk and Dubai with Uber are pioneering the future regulatory environment. Things to consider are whether autonomy can be made reliable, whether a pilot's licence is necessary and what airspace can be used. Then, infrastructure must be built in terms of takeoff and landing zones, charging, predefined flight corridors and air traffic control, before flying cars can become commonplace.

An artist's conception of a self-driving passenger drone.

# Computing and artificial intelligence (AI)

Until the mid-20th century, a computer was a person who performed mathematical calculations. Charles Babbage and Ada Lovelace laid some foundations of automation and programming before, in 1936, Alan Turing hypothesized a universal machine – a computer – that could execute any programmable task. Working at Bletchley Park during World War II, Turing helped turn some of his theory into practice, contributing to code-breaking machines Bombe and Colossus.

A world without computers is hard to imagine. Miniaturization through integrated circuits has made them ubiquitous and increasingly invisible. In 1950, Turing asked the question, 'Can machines think?' We've already delegated tasks such as flying aeroplanes and driving cars. In the future computers will take over many more cognitive tasks, including creating works of art and making original contributions to science, perhaps through deep insights into the Universe. They will even develop methods by which humans and machines can travel to the stars.

Slate statue of mathematician Alan Turing at Bletchley Park.

# Moore's law

In 1965, Intel co-founder Gordon Moore identified that the number of transistors on a chip had doubled every two years and forecast this would continue. What Caltech professor Carver Mead christened 'Moore's law' has taken many forms, including David House, another Intel executive, suggesting computers 'double in speed' every 18 months. He was almost spot on – half a century on, the rate is around every 20 months. Doubling matters on long timescales. In 2000 computers were two million times more powerful than in 1965, but by 2020 that figure will be over seven billion. By 2058, computers will be a million times more powerful again. Moore himself said 'no physical quantity can continue to change exponentially forever', but it doesn't have to. Economics is the driver and industry focus has switched to graphics processors using clever computer architecture for faster calculations. Even as natural physical limits come into view with one technology, new approaches such as quantum (see page 120) and DNA computing (see page 122) will drive the future forward.

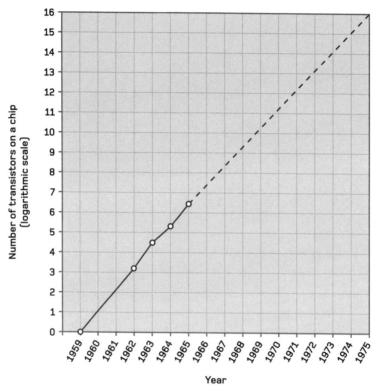

Gordon Moore's 'Cramming more components onto integrated circuits' appeared in *Electronics* magazine.

# Big data

The Sloan Digital Sky Survey to map the Universe collected more data in its first weeks in 2000 than has been produced during the previous history of astronomy. Networking company Cisco says web traffic grew 568 times between 2000 and 2014, all recorded and analyzed. This data deluge is quickening – sensors on fully autonomous vehicles alone will generate more than 300TB per vehicle annually. Big data helps reveal new and deeper insights. Machine learning (see page 116) uses small portions of these datasets to train computers before analysing the rest of the information using AI – every day our records are scored to see if we'll default on credit or switch phone providers. Future uses may be to explore datasets to identify possible Earth-like planets beyond the solar system. Analytics is the process of examining the huge datasets to uncover patterns and correlations. In the future this will help us to optimize crop yields and may ultimately lead to new and profound ways of predicting human behaviour. With no near-term limit to memory storage and processing, data will just get bigger in the future.

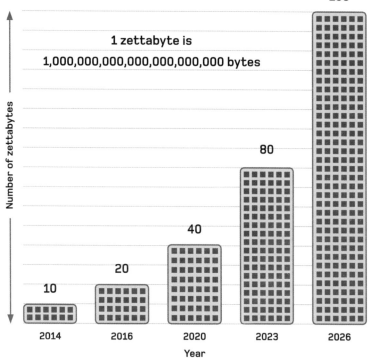

Projected doubling of the global data sphere.

# Algorithms

An algorithm is a set of instructions to be performed in a specific order, not unlike a recipe in a cookbook. 'Code' is the implementation of an algorithm in a specific computer language. Ada Lovelace said it was essential 'to choose that arrangement which shall tend to reduce to a minimum the time necessary for completing the calculation' and improvements in algorithmic design have had impact orders of magnitude bigger than Moore's law.

With the rise of machine learning, algorithmic bias has become a prominent societal issue, highlighted by Wall Street quantitative analyst Cathy O'Neil. In her book *Weapons of Math Destruction*, O'Neil cites an automated soap dispenser not working for black people because the algorithms weren't trained across all skin tones as just one example as to why unconscious programmer bias must be addressed. Looking further ahead, smarter machines will rewrite their own algorithms by a process known as 'recursive self-improvement' that has the potential to lead to an intelligence explosion (see page 332).

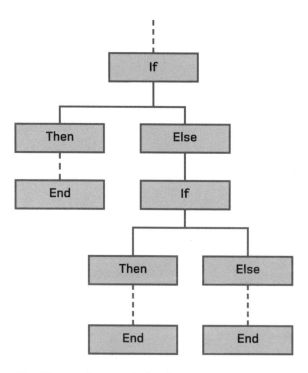

Algorithms can be presented as flow charts made up of
boxes representing steps, inputs and outputs. If/then/else
algorithms occur frequently in computer programming.

# Open source

Should the future of computing be that of fenced-off realms, staked out by private enterprise and government, or collaborative ventures to which many contribute? The latter, termed 'open source', began in the 1990s when a free operating system for PCs, called Linux, went into direct competition with Microsoft's Windows. When Wikipedia started, few believed a web encyclopedia written by volunteers could be more reliable than major reference works such as Britannica – Wikipedia won decisively. In 2018, 12% of cell phones ran Apple's closed iOS software within a fiercely protected closed ecosystem, with 88% on Google's semi-open-source Android – yet Apple's branding and pricing made it the more valuable company. The transparency of open source matters to future privacy champions because experts can view the code to ensure it's not spying on you. Proprietary software is a black box in comparison. But perhaps the biggest future contribution will come from organizations such as OpenAI, producing software tools to accelerate AI research, in a transparent and safe way, helping to solve the control problem.

A champion of software freedom, the Open Source Initiative (logo pictured) is a global non-profit organization that protects and promotes open-source software, development and communities.

# Artificial intelligence (AI)

In the introduction to his 1950 'imitation game', now called the Turing Test, Alan Turing posed the question 'Can machines think?'. Turing pondered machines of human-level intelligence, but in 1965 his collaborator Irving Good took the next logical step, hypothesizing the creation of an 'ultraintelligent machine'. AI dominates discussions about the future. Machine learning is a subset of AI techniques that uses big data (see page 110) – for example, training computers on thousands of examples of 'fraudulent transactions' in credit card data so machines learn how to identify them. A popular machine-learning technique uses 'deep neural networks' to mimic brain architecture through a hierarchy of artificial neurons for tasks such as speech recognition. A computer's speed is measured in 'flops' (floating point operations per second). It's estimated the human brain works at anywhere between $10^{13}$ to $10^{25}$ flops; futurist Ray Kurzweil uses these numbers to predict machines will equal the thinking power of a single human brain by 2029, and that of all humans by 2045, ushering in The Singularity (see page 316).

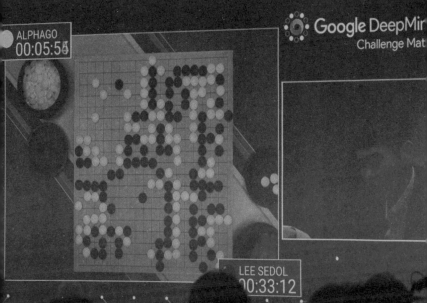

ALPHAGO
00:05:54

Google DeepMir
Challenge Mat

LEE SEDOL
00:33:12

The Google DeepMind Challenge Match took place in Seoul, South Korea, in March 2016. Eighteen-time world Go champion Lee Sedol took on the computer program AlphaGo, developed by Google DeepMind. The match involved five games of which AlphaGo won all but the fourth.

# Bayesian reasoning

Bayes' theorem is a mathematical rule for updating what we think we know on the basis of new evidence. If a coin toss comes up heads 20 times in a row, Bayesians might conclude it's biased rather than thinking this was simply unlikely, as opposed to traditional 'frequentist' statistics which deal in absolute or objective probabilities. Bayesian techniques need powerful computers, but with the emergence of artificial general intelligence (AGI) the future of statistics and how machines reach their conclusions will be firmly Bayesian. Currently AI is described as 'narrow' since it relates to specific application domains; AGI would demonstrate intelligence in multiple areas, like a human. AGIs will combine what they know with utility functions (see page 318) to test which course of action is best. For example, given finite resources to spend on global water purification, malaria prevention and reduction of carbon dioxide emissions, a computer will use Bayesian techniques to predict the outcomes of different courses of action before deciding what resources to allocate to each problem.

$$P(A|B) = \frac{P(B|A)P(A)}{P(B)}$$

Bayes' theorem was devised by the
Reverend Thomas Bayes. It tells us
the updated probability of an event A,
given the knowledge that B has occurred.

# Quantum computing

With the United States, European Union and China pouring tens of billions of dollars of research funding into quantum computing, technology looks set to undergo an enormous boost. While a traditional computer bit can be a one or a zero, a quantum bit ('qubit') is in a superposition of both states, until observed. Two qubits are in a superposition of four states and generally $n$ qubits are the equivalent of $2^n$ regular bits, meaning just 20 qubits can do the equivalent work of more than one million regular bits. Current quantum processors have qubits numbering in the low hundreds, but are too fleetingly stable to be useful; a genuine quantum computer will need a few thousand more. Google, IBM, Microsoft and others are working on quantum chips that may see a bona fide quantum computer by 2030 with consumer versions arriving in the 2050s. Among the subjects that lend themselves to quantum computation is the chemistry of molecules. Understanding these will enable more efficient batteries. Another area is encryption, with corporations and governments rushing to devise quantum-proof techniques. Further ahead it may be a stepping stone towards AGI.

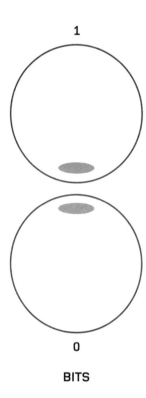

**BITS**

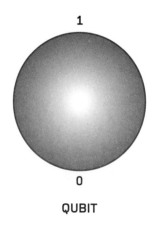

**QUBIT**

A classical computer bit takes the value 1 or a 0 (each a single point on a 'Bloch sphere'); between measurements a qubit can be in a superposition of classical states and anywhere within the sphere.

# DNA computing

At the University of Southern California in 1994, Leonard Adleman used DNA instead of traditional silicon to perform computations. The two DNA base pairs lend themselves to computation as alternatives to ones and zeroes. With the rise of big data, DNA could become the solution to storage problems – Microsoft researchers have shown $1mm^3$ of DNA can theoretically store an exabyte (a billion gigabytes) of data for thousands of years without degrading. Because of its organic nature, DNA has the potential to store synaptic activity and become an external hard drive for memories. Classical computers are deterministic universal Turing machines, always taking the same action given the same input, while non-deterministic machines have many potential outputs. Manchester University's Ross King foresees that 'a desktop DNA non-deterministic Turing machine could potentially utilize more processors than all the electronic computers in the world combined, and thereby outperform the world's current fastest supercomputer, while consuming a tiny fraction of its energy.'

## Encoded GIF

## Recalled GIF

In 2017, Harvard scientists encoded Eadweard Muybridge's galloping horse pictures into synthetic DNA, successfully retrieving the video below.

# Internet of humans

Instead of controlling the Internet of things through clumsy external interfaces, such as when swiping a cell phone screen, humans will become central nodes in a future with ubiquitous sensors. Imminently, more than half the commands to cell phones will be spoken, introducing an era in which we will control devices increasingly through simple gestures, and ultimately via neural interfaces (see page 288). Inertial measurement units (IMUs) are sensors that combine accelerometers, gyroscopes and magnetometers. Joseph Paradiso at the MIT Media Lab describes the path to this future beginning in the next few years with wrist-worn IMUs providing precise indoor location, and adding cameras, temperature and humidity sensors and microphones as necessary. With humans integrated into the web of data, privacy and security issues will come to the fore with the protection of digital identities paramount. Instead of corporations owning our data, the future could return control to individuals, using biometric blockchain-based encryption and determining, and charging for, access as desired.

# The environment

Humans have impacted the environment throughout history, clearing land for grazing and crop planting. Earth today is very different to that of a few millennia ago, which was different again from that of our hunter-gatherer forebears.

Through the 21st century the environment will be under great strain. American ecologist David Tilman forecasts that, by 2050, demand for food from a larger and wealthier global population will mean an area of natural environment bigger than the United States must be turned over to agriculture, with massive increases in fertilizer and pesticide use, and twice as much fresh water for irrigation. He sees this leading to 'unprecedented ecosystem simplification, loss of ecosystem services, and species extinction'. To preserve the potential value of human lives in the future, we must be able to live well on Earth, so it's incumbent on us to be good stewards of our planet and find solutions to see us through the coming decades of peak population and climate change.

The Blue Marble image of Earth, taken by astronauts aboard Apollo 17 in 1972.

# Pollution

**A** 2007 World Bank study is thought to have put pollution-related deaths in China alone at around one million a year, due to poor air and water quality. This led to China massively investing in renewable technologies. Earlier Western clean air acts have seen dramatic falls in levels of common pollutants, but the rise in urban traffic has made future targets difficult to achieve – hence timelines for banning new diesel and petrol vehicles (in Norway by 2025 and France and the United Kingdom by 2040).

The 20th century saw the development of incredible plastics, but in the 21st we face their polluting legacy in our seas and landfills. The 2017 UN Environment Assembly noted that 4.8 to 12.7 million tonnes of plastic find their way into the oceans annually, creating areas such as the Great Pacific Garbage Patch. Dutch company The Ocean Cleanup is developing autonomous technologies that could lead to plastic-free ocean surfaces by 2050, but more work is urgently needed to clear ocean depths and the food chain of these pollutants.

# Waste and recycling

**B**angladesh began the ban on thin plastic bags in 2002; dozens of nations followed suit, with many single-use plastics to be phased out in the coming years. In 2018, pollution worries meant China ended its policy of accepting Western plastic waste for recycling. Countries managing their own waste need to make it more efficient; it is no longer acceptable to simply bury or burn it. Europe alone has half a million landfill sites and waste-management companies have begun mining these to recover useful metals, such as lithium, as their prices rise. Plastics, textiles and wood will also increasingly be transformed into energy, using designer microbes to convert them into biofuels. By far the best future waste and recycling strategy is not to produce waste at all, but to build sustainability into product design. Additive manufacturing will help, reusing base materials (for instance when printing new clothes, see page 58), as will a more modular strategy for consumer goods, exemplified by the Fairphone project, which shows how products can evolve rather than be discarded.

Fairphone, the world's first ethical, modular smartphone.

# Scarcity

Uri Neren, from the World Database of Innovation, names scarcity as the number one factor in almost all creative problem-solving. Economics dictates that as a material becomes scarcer, its price rises. Where a once-cheap raw material was vital, industry innovates to replace the old with new technologies. The concept of 'peak oil' – when more than half of the world's oil has been extracted, predicted around 2030 – demonstrates this with the dramatic move towards sustainable transport. Scarcity is relative, defined by our knowledge. If the only way to power a car were the internal combustion engine we might want to ration gasoline; now we know how to make electric vehicles, lithium may become scarce – making us find innovative sources or invent better batteries (see page 160). Also, future resources should not be limited to what's only available on our home planet. Asteroid mining (see page 340) will be an enormous growth industry from the 2030s onwards, helping lead to the industrialization of space and de-industrialization of Earth, making scarcity on our homeworld far less of a future concern.

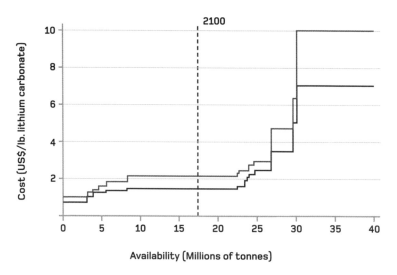

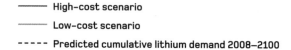

Legend:
High-cost scenario
Low-cost scenario
Predicted cumulative lithium demand 2008–2100

As the cumulative amount of lithium extracted reaches approximately
23 million tonnes, it becomes scarce and the price rises sharply to a ceiling
(at 30 million tonnes) when it becomes more cost-effective to extract
from seawater than other techniques.

# Sustainability

In 2018, Mathis Wackernagel, CEO of Global Footprint Network, claimed that civilization had exceeded Earth's 'carrying capacity' (Earth's ability to replenish resources as we use them) by 70%. Many believe civilization in its current form is unsustainable – American ecological economist Herman Daly argues for immediate government rationing, ignoring that human society is not limited by Earth's resources. We can continue to exploit nature's bounty to drive economic and technological progress, but only by becoming spacefaring. A popular argument for sustainability involves finding ways to use a lot less to do more – such as generating more energy with fewer emissions. This approach hopes to create both a sustainable and prosperous future, but many are sceptical. If it can't be done, a team of UN environmental scientists predicts that, by 2050, global society will be using three times the mineral resources consumed in 2010. As the world becomes wealthier and consumes more, it is sensible to reduce resource intensity to buy humanity time until we can access resources beyond Earth.

The electric light has driven human progress but the transition to ever more energy-saving designs has slashed global energy demand, reducing carbon emissions.

# Climate change

In the 1920s, Serbian astrophysicist Milutin Milankovitch proposed the generally accepted theory that climate change of the past had much to do with three astronomical 'Milankovitch cycles': the eccentricity of Earth's orbit; Earth's axial tilt; and Earth's precession (how much it 'wobbles' on its axis). The Industrial Revolution added a fourth, anthropogenic element, raising atmospheric levels of greenhouse gas carbon dioxide ($CO_2$) from 280 parts per million to 410 by 2018. Of the 18 warmest years in the 136-year record, 17 occurred between 2001 and 2017. Despite action to reduce $CO_2$ the International Governmental Panel on Climate Change anticipates a rise in mean global temperature of 0.3 to 0.7°C by 2035. Reducing $CO_2$ emissions impacts both their 2050 and 2100 projections, and the efforts to hold temperature rises to 2°C above preindustrial levels. Human civilization has flourished since the end of the last glaciation because we have lived through a time of remarkable climate stability. As this changes, we face an uncertain future with less cultivable land and drinking water, more extreme weather, but billions more humans.

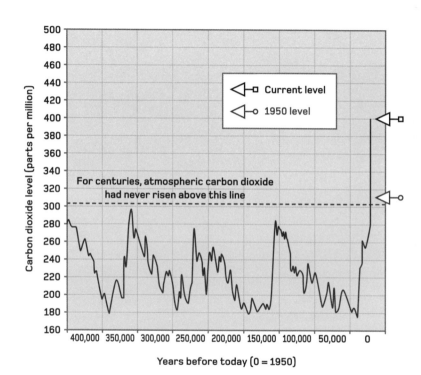

Based on the comparison of atmospheric samples contained in ice cores and more recent direct measurements, this graph shows how atmospheric $CO_2$ has increased since the Industrial Revolution.

# Biodiversity

Biodiversity, the variety of living things, matters both for maintaining our food supply and creating new pharmaceuticals. Environmental scientist Bill Laurance says 'rapid disruption of tropical forests probably imperils global biodiversity more than any other contemporary phenomenon' and argues for greater protection of these and surrounding areas. The WWF predicts 27% of the Amazon biome will be without trees by 2030 if current deforestation continues; it also lists some rhinos, tigers, gorillas, orangutans and elephants as 'critically endangered'. Stanford biologist Anthony Barnosky has investigated the claim of many that we are living through Earth's sixth mass extinction event, (the fifth wiping out the dinosaurs). He concludes that current rates are highly elevated and, were they to continue through to 2400, this era would qualify as a mass extinction. The reason for extinction is habitat loss, but over coming centuries climate change will play an increasing role as species struggle to adapt to dramatically different local conditions. Future genetic zoos may preserve species' DNA until climate change can be reversed.

The Global Seed Vault.
Buried inside a mountain on
the Arctic island of Svalbard,
its contents has been built to
maintain crop diversity in the
event of biodiversity loss.

# The ice-free Arctic

The Holocene began as the ice sheets retreated nearly 12,000 years ago, but ice remained at Earth's poles. The Northwest Passage, first navigated by Norwegian Roald Amundsen between 1903 and 1906, was declared open in 2007, making shipping possible some of the year. The 1981 to 2010 Arctic average saw 11 million km² sea ice in winter retreat to just under 7 million km² in summer (4.25 to 3 million square miles). Arctic temperatures have soared at four times global rates, melting permafrost to release trapped methane (a stronger greenhouse gas than $CO_2$).

Seeing the Blue Marble Earth missing a polar cap could prove a pivotal moment in perceptions of climate change. Arctic expert Alexandra Jahn gives a range of 2032 to 2058 for when the Arctic will become ice free for the first time, with a consecutive decade of ice-free summers likely to begin between 2040 and 2064 if $CO_2$ emissions are not reduced. But because the Sun is below the horizon during winter, the transition to a year-round ice-free Arctic will not happen in the foreseeable future.

Ice is highly reflective whereas dark seawater absorbs the Sun's rays, so melting ice is an amplifying feedback.

# Sea-level rise

What matters for future rising sea levels is the melting of ice over land. The Greenland Ice Sheet (GIS) contains 8% of Earth's ice – were all of this to melt, global sea levels would rise 6m (19½ft). If the West Antarctic Ice Sheet (WAIS) melted, sea levels would rise 3.2m (10½ft); if the huge East Antarctic Ice Sheet (EAIS) melted, the rise would be 60m (197ft). In 2017, a Dartmouth College team showed the GIS was melting at its fastest rate since at least 1550. In 2018, a massive international investigation revealed the WAIS was melting three times faster than its baseline figure. The Intergovernmental Panel on Climate Change (IPCC) forecasts range from 53–117cm (21–46in) by 2100, with sea levels likely to continue to rise through to 2300, possibly with the complete loss of the GIS. With rising, warming oceans also comes the risk of storm surges. According to the Organization for Economic Co-operation and Development (OECD), Asia is most vulnerable in terms of coastal population centres at risk, with Miami, Greater New York City and New Orleans all making the top ten.

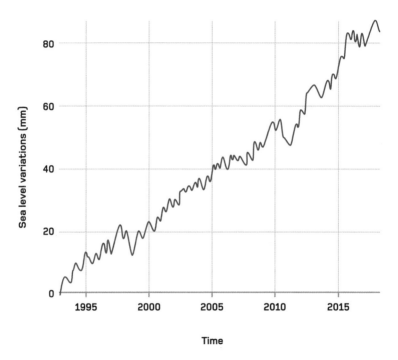

Changes in sea level since 1993 as observed by satellites.

# Food supply

Thomas Malthus's 1798 book *An Essay on the Principle of Population* defined the relationship between food supply and population. To feed a wealthier, urbanized population of at least nine billion by 2050, the 2009 World Food Summit concluded that we will need to produce 70% more food. Currently, more than three-quarters of the 51 million $km^2$ (19.5 million square miles) given over to agriculture are used to raise livestock with less than one-quarter for crops, yet crops provide most of our calorie and protein intake. Transitioning from a meat-dominated diet (see page 48) should be a practical as well as moral future choice. Our crops have evolved in a period of great climate stability. Genetically modified organisms (GMOs), such as cassava and rice, can help in a transition to a warmer, wetter world, with scientists now engineering for higher yields through more efficient photosynthesis. Although standard elsewhere, GMOs remain banned in the EU due to consumer pressure. Further, in 2018 the European Commission banned foods modified using CRISPR gene editing (see page 248), against scientific advice.

GMO canola crops.

# Water supply

By 2025, 1.8 billion people will have no access to clean water. By 2030, the US intelligence community reports that water demand will be 40% above sustainable supply, with great stress in North Africa, the Middle East and Asia. Only 0.3% of Earth's water resides in lakes, rivers and wetlands, but Earth has oceans. In 2016, desalination provided around 1% of drinking water, with high cost a barrier, but China (home to one-fifth of the world's population with only 7% of its available freshwater) plans to use it to produce three million tonnes of freshwater every day by 2020. By 2023, Israel will be the first country self-sufficient in desalinated water. Existing plants work by 'reverse osmosis', but to satisfy future needs, desalination requires breakthrough technology. Manchester materials scientist Rahul Nair is promoting graphene for desalination, but the material remains in its infancy and industrial implementation is decades away. Further ahead, the era of radical abundance will enable work at the molecular level (see page 372), producing much more efficient membranes to help solve human water needs using this technology.

# Reverse osmosis

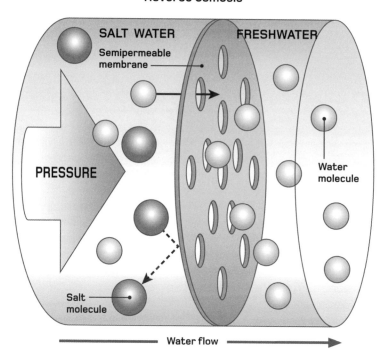

Reverse osmosis involves forcing salt water through a membrane with holes too small for the salt molecules to pass through, producing freshwater as a result.

# Climate geoengineering

Climate geoengineering means intentionally affecting Earth's atmosphere on a planetary scale. When Mount Pinatubo in the Philippines erupted in 1991, it temporarily lowered global temperatures by half a degree. Mimicking the effect, it's proposed that pumping sulfur aerosols into the upper atmosphere will reflect sunlight and reduce temperatures through this 'volcanic winter' effect. Downsides are that temperatures rebound as soon as the process is halted and sulfur damages the ozone layer. But this could be a low-cost emergency measure to buy time for more permanent action. High-tech approaches involve albedo enhancers (making areas of Earth's surface or clouds more reflective) or space-based reflectors (preventing some solar radiation even reaching the atmosphere). Some environmentalists see this as an excuse for not reducing greenhouse gas emissions, while advocates stress it should complement aggressive reduction targets. To keep to the official IPCC target of a minimum 2°C temperature rise by 2100, opinions vary between 2022 and 2045 for when a programme would need to begin.

# Principle of a space lens

A space-based lens could disperse light on a path to Earth,
reducing incoming solar radiation and lowering temperatures.

# Fuelling the future

Between 2000 and 2017, global energy consumption rose 41%. Without phasing out incandescent lightbulbs, it would have been over 50%. Our insatiable appetite for power has led to us affecting the climate of our planet (see page 136). American strategic consultants McKinsey & Company predict our hunger will slow and world consumption in 2050 will 'only' be 150% greater than 2010, due to global efficiency improvements such as passive design to heat and cool buildings. Our use of fossil fuels may have risked the planet, but the strides we have taken in terms of wealth and health, art and science, suggest the gamble was worth taking. Having used up much of the fossil fuel reserves and risked the climate, future societies will not have the same opportunity. Building a sustainable future becomes increasingly important as we balance the needs of the biosphere with the moral imperative to maximize the value of future lives, but it would be a mistake to do this in a way that jeopardizes the potential spacefaring future (see page 334) that our use of fossil fuels has brought within reach.

All our energy originates from the Sun. Fossil fuels represent the Sun's energy condensed during millions of years that we have been busy burning through in just decades since the Industrial Revolution.

# Wind power

Throughout the first millennium BCE, Persian civilization used wind power for pumping water and grinding grain. Around 1000 CE, the technology spread to Europe, the Dutch employing it to drain the Rhine delta. In 1893, at the Chicago World Fair, 15 companies exhibited wind turbines for electricity generation, but use of wind power has waxed and waned. Climate change created the modern demand for wind farms, with global wind power generation increasing 25-fold between 2000 and 2015. Chinese generation accounts for 40% of today's global capacity, and the United States targets wind to provide 20% of its own generation capacity by 2030. The price is falling everywhere to the extent that the first contracts have been awarded for offshore wind without government subsidies. This is the area of biggest potential – Dutch provider TenneT proposes an artificial island in the North Sea at some point beyond 2030 to act as a transnational hub for offshore wind generation. By that time, offshore windmills will have become supersized with today's 80m (260ft) turbines growing to 125m (410ft) with blades 190m (625ft) in diameter.

An artist's impression of the TenneT artificial island.

# Solar power

Solar panels comprise large numbers of photovoltaic cells, in which particles of light (photons) free electrons from silicon to generate electricity. In 2016, solar power became the fastest-growing means of electricity generation, China accounting for nearly half the new solar panels installed. International Energy Authority projections have solar power rising over 400% between 2020 and 2050, by which time Bloomberg predicts that solar and wind combined will account for half the world's power generation. More efficient panels, smarter grid connections, the addition of organic technology (plants use solar power in photosynthesis), and new nanomaterials will all drive innovation. The Desertec project proposed to carpet the Sahara with panels to fulfil the energy requirements of North Africa, the Middle East and Europe, but stalled due to geopolitical considerations. In an uncertain future, developed nations are also likely to embark on more secure and controllable space-based solar power collectors, on which the Sun shines 24 hours a day, though this will only likely be practicable once asteroid mining becomes an established technology (see page 340).

The Desert Sunlight Solar Farm in the Mojave Desert, California. It uses approximately 8.8 million cadmium telluride modules.

# Other renewables

The futures of smart grids (see page 158) and renewables such as wind and sun are interconnected. While wind and solar will dominate, hydro, wave, tidal, geothermal and novel biofuels, such as that generated from algae, will have a part to play. Wood-burning has major potential, but any claims that it is carbon-neutral are contentious, and many synthetic biofuels compete with land for crop growing. Brazil and China currently dominate the hydroelectric scene, the former generating 70% of its electricity this way and the latter's Three Gorges Dam being the world's largest. Because water is so much denser than air to drive turbines, wave power or more predictable tidal barrages have long been touted, but engineering difficulties have meant slow takeup. Six nations currently generate more than 15% of their electricity using geothermal energy, Iceland having the highest percentage. Ironically, flooded disused coalmines are being proposed as future geothermal power sources. Geothermal energy may provide 3 to 5% of global generation by 2050, and up to 10% by 2100.

The Nesjavellir Geothermal Power Plant in Iceland.

# Smart grids

A smart grid is the future evolution of the traditional electricity grid, providing a more secure, flexible and dependable service. It connects traditional power stations, but also renewables from macro (eg, offshore wind plants) and microgeneration (eg, solar panels on a roof). While traditional grids were one-way, smart grids provide constant two-way communication. With electricity and information flowing in all directions, utilities will be continuously aware of demand and even the reason for changes, perhaps as an electric vehicle is recharging or if the Sun goes behind clouds. With microgenerated renewables connected, smart grids will be more resilient and better prepared to address emergencies such as severe storms, earthquakes, large solar flares or terrorist attacks, due to automatic rerouting when equipment fails or outages occur. If necessary, power resupply can be prioritized for emergency services. Consumers will have unprecedented control of their own energy supply. Information is a key future resource and smart grids will be just one part of smart cities (see page 90).

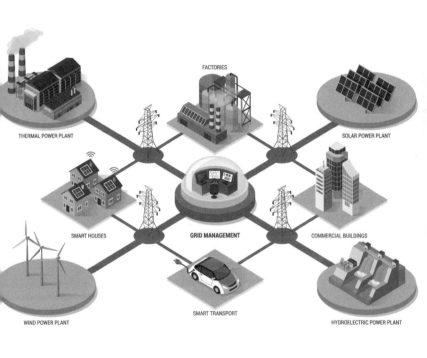

FACTORIES

THERMAL POWER PLANT

SOLAR POWER PLANT

SMART HOUSES

GRID MANAGEMENT

COMMERCIAL BUILDINGS

WIND POWER PLANT

SMART TRANSPORT

HYDROELECTRIC POWER PLANT

# Energy storage

Most renewables are unpredictable and cannot store surplus energy, so storing energy, say, whenever the wind is blowing, is key. Hydroelectric projects enable storage as potential energy of water in a raised reservoir, generating power during peak demand, before pumping water back uphill into its 'storage position' using off-peak cheaper electricity.

Battery technology will be key to future energy storage. Lithium-ion technology provides the current rechargeable battery of choice. Tesla's Nevada Gigafactory will become the largest building in the world on completion, producing half the world's lithium-ion batteries. By 2018, Tesla had installed over 1 GWh (enough to boil 10,000 full kettles) of energy storage in storage in Australia and Puerto Rico using its Powerwalls. Research on future batteries is a massive global enterprise, with liquid metal, metal–air, lithium–sulfur, solid-state metal-anode, and also graphene all contenders for next and next-but-one generation batteries to enable a greener, more convenient future.

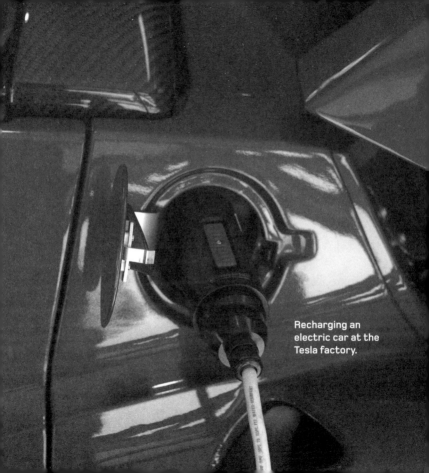

Recharging an
electric car at the
Tesla factory.

# Carbon capture and storage

As more power is generated through fossil fuels, more $CO_2$ is released. If attempts to cut emissions fail, or are insufficient to prevent a warming world, carbon capture and storage are two speculative technologies that may help to protect the environment. The first captures $CO_2$ released at source by power stations; the second sucks it from the atmosphere and oceans. Of the two, capture at source is more efficient due to the higher concentrations. NET Power has demonstrated a trial facility at a Texan gas-fired power plant and plans a larger-scale rollout in the 2020s. Removal of $CO_2$ from the atmosphere is a form of climate geoengineering (see page 148). Technological solutions are in their infancy, though one machine already exists – the tree. Future reforestation programmes could play a role, but Columbia University's Wally Broecker and Klaus Lackner have gone further, researching artificial trees that are a thousand times more efficient. Using a plastic resin, Lacker estimates 20 million of his creations would be sufficient to extract one part per million (see page 136) of $CO_2$ from the atmosphere.

Trees are nature's way of removing $CO_2$ from the atmosphere.

# Nuclear fusion through Tokamaks

Ever since hydrogen bombs were first tested, nations have been working towards the peaceful use of nuclear fusion for electricity generation – traditionally estimated 30 years in the future. The consensus has been to achieve this using Tokamaks. Invented by Russians Andrei Sakharov and Igor Tamm in the 1950s, these are doughnut-shaped devices that use very powerful magnets to confine high-temperature plasmas. International collaborations hope to scale the technology into working fusion reactors. The project started in 1977 with the Joint European Torus in Oxfordshire, and follows a roadmap that finally hopes to see fusion power generated on a commercial basis between 2055 and 2060. Many believe it is taking too long. MIT spinoff Commonwealth Fusion Systems – backed by Jeff Bezos, Bill Gates and Richard Branson – aims to produce net energy by 2025 and to start contributing to the grid a decade later, using new superconducting magnets to enable the building of smaller affordable, robust, compact Tokamaks known as ARCs.

The ITER Tokamak in southern France is scheduled for completion in 2025, with full-scale experiments planned for 2035. The very small man (bottom left) gives an idea of the scale.

# Other routes to nuclear fusion

In recent decades, alongside research in Tokamaks, scientists have begun to examine other potential routes to fusion. For example, at labs such as Lawrence Livermore's National Ignition Facility, research into inertial-confinement fusion proposes that small fusible fuel pellets, raised to very high temperatures using lasers, become compressed to generate energy.

Numerous startups have more radical approaches. British Columbia's General Fusion is 3D-printing reactor components and using data analytics to inject plasmas into liquid metal cavities. TAE Technologies has raised nearly one billion dollars to attempt hydrogen–boron 'friendly fusion', while Washington's Agni Energy is attempting beam-target fusion, bombarding a tritium target with deuterium. Despite the rise of renewables, fusion will likely be necessary for humanity to fulfil its potential, allowing limitless cheap energy on Earth while powering outer solar system colonies and generational starships (see page 358).

The preamplifiers of the National Ignition Facility. In 2012 they achieved a 500 terawatt shot — 1,000 times more power than the United States uses at any instant in time.

# Nuclear fission with thorium

Nuclear fission creates energy by splitting heavy atoms into smaller ones. Conventionally, the fuel is uranium-235 or plutonium-239. By-products are highly radioactive and remain so for thousands of years. Catastrophic 'meltdown' was narrowly avoided in fission plants at Chernobyl, Three Mile Island and Fukushima.

Following Fukushima in 2011, Georgia Tech scientists proposed fission power using thorium-232 that wouldn't risk meltdown. An experimental thorium reactor operated at Oak Ridge from 1965 to 1969 but research was discontinued. Startup costs for a new fission reactor are huge, but the future benefits great. India (with large thorium reserves) has set a target of generating 30% of its electricity through thorium fission by 2050. China has begun a research programme, officially partnering with Oak Ridge. The Georgia Tech authors describe it as 'a 1000+ year solution or a quality low-carbon bridge to truly sustainable energy sources solving a huge portion of mankind's negative environmental impact'.

In 2011, a massive earthquake off the coast of Japan caused a tsunami that engulfed the nuclear power plant at Fukushima, disabling the emergency generators designed to cool the reactors and risking nuclear 'meltdown'. Such a potential disaster is not possible using thorium nuclear power.

# Dyson swarms

In 1960 physicist Freeman Dyson suggested that any sufficiently advanced extraterrestrial civilization under pressure to generate energy would dismantle planets and build gigantic hollow spheres to encompass and capture the entire output of its parent star. Dyson's paper was intended to find a way to detect aliens; an immediate clarification was that a sphere would not be stable, but that 'swarms' of space habitats and solar collectors orbiting the star would generate power and detectable infrared signatures. Dyson suggested human society would need to do this in around 3,000 years. Others have proposed we begin sooner. In 2012, Oxford physicist Stuart Armstrong suggested using self-replicating robotic space assemblers to mine the planet Mercury as a way of producing a partial Dyson swarm incrementally and economically over a period of half a century. Canadian futurist George Dworsky favours dismantling Mercury in its entirety, while others suggest future humans would be better served creating a Dyson swarm using asteroids.

A Dyson sphere would have more than 500 million times the
surface area of Earth and could collect all of the Sun's energy.

# Kardashev scale

How much energy we might use further into the future was defined by Russian astrophysicist Nikolai Kardashev in his 1964 paper 'Transmission of Information by Extraterrestrial Civilizations', sketching what has become known as the Kardashev scale of Types I, II and III civilizations.

A Type I civilization would use all the energy available on its home planet through radiation from its parent star. Cosmologist Carl Sagan positioned humans at 0.7 on this scale in the 1970s while physicist Michio Kaku suggests humans will reach Type I in one or two centuries. Type II is when a civilization is so advanced it is able to harness all the energy available from a star, an example of which would be a Dyson swarm. Type III uses and controls all the energy output of a galaxy, a simple example perhaps being in the form of billions of Dyson swarms. The scale has been extended to accommodate the possibility of a future civilization controlling the energy of the entire Universe (Type IV) and of multiple universes (Type V).

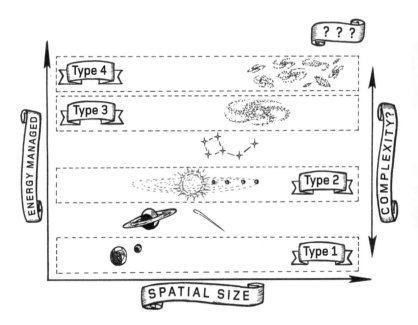

The Kardashev scale

# Matter/antimatter burners

Nuclear fission and fusion make use of Einstein's $E = mc^2$, transforming matter into energy. Although each releases vast quantities of energy (because $c$, the speed of light, is so large) the amount of matter converted is a tiny proportion of the overall mass of the atoms involved (since they are being transformed into different atoms). The most efficient process of energy creation in the Universe would be matter/antimatter burning in which the full potential of Einstein's equation is realized. Antimatter is where fundamental particles carry the opposite electrical charge to normal. For reasons that are uncertain, the Universe seems to consist almost exclusively of matter, but we do create small quantities of antimatter in particle accelerators. Serbian astronomer Milan Ćirković suggests a way to observe extraterrestrial intelligences would be to look for signatures from matter/antimatter burners. In the very far future, what has become of human civilization could store antimatter using magnetic fields and bring it into controlled contact with matter to power civilizations or advanced starships.

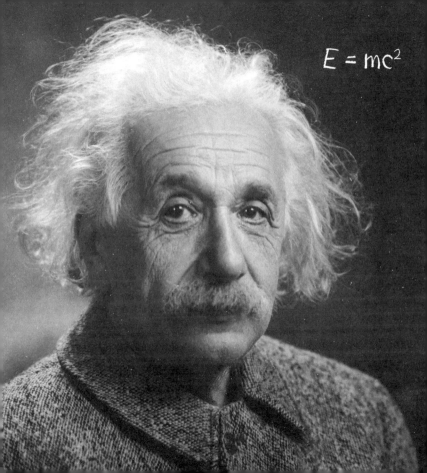

# Black holes

A black hole, predicted in Einstein's theory of general relativity, is an object so dense that its gravity is strong enough to prevent light (or anything else) escaping once beyond the hole's 'event horizon'.

The theory was developed by British physicists Stephen Hawking and Roger Penrose, and the 'Penrose process' describes how a very advanced civilization might extract enormous quantities of energy from a rotating black hole. Careful arrangement of material close to the event horizon allows some matter to escape with extra energy, which can then be captured. By this method, a theoretical 29% of the original mass of the black hole could be converted into energy, this limit because the process reduces the black hole's angular momentum until it stops rotating altogether. Through a similar process with electrically charged rotating black holes, Roger Blandford and Roman Znajek estimate that, in one second, a black hole eight times more massive than our Sun would supply as much energy as global society currently consumes in a year.

Stephen Hawking suggested finding or even creating micro black holes as a future power source, positioning them in Earth orbit.

# Changing ethics

Many historic empires have been built on slavery. Until the American Civil War, the Constitution considered a slave to be worth just three-fifths of a free person. The vote came slowly to women. In many parts of the world it is still considered the business of the state as to what gender of person someone can be allowed to love.

Presentism uncritically holds the past to the moral standards of the day, and always finds it wanting. In the same way, values we hold dear will be considered outrageous by our descendants – as their world may appal us. Regarding incels (involuntary celibates), economist Robin Hanson asked, 'If we are concerned about the just distribution of property and money, why do we assume that the desire for some sort of sexual redistribution is inherently ridiculous?' The future world of automation raises new questions about the right not to have your job, and perhaps purpose, taken by a machine. And as those machines become more intelligent, should they have rights, too (see page 200)?

# Inequality

In 1912, Italian statistician Corrado Gini devised a coefficient of wealth distribution where 0 represents perfect equality while 100% is a very unequal society. Economists Tomá Hellebrandt and Paolo Mauro report the world's Gini coefficient fell from 69% in 2003 to 65% a decade later, and forecast that by 2035 it will be 61%. Yet since the 2008 financial crisis, the richest 1% have become significantly richer – by 2030 they'll have two-thirds of the world's wealth. To aid equality, many technology leaders are signing up to the 2017 Asilomar Principles for beneficial artificial intelligence (AI), including that 'AI technologies should benefit and empower as many people as possible' and that 'the economic prosperity created by AI should be shared broadly, to benefit all of humanity'. Universal basic income (see page 44) may be one route towards that, but once some humans become enhanced, will others be capable of being their equals? American bioethicist James Hughes says, 'The more ability we have as individuals, the better we become', so that enhancement will give us the drive as well as the ability to end the political problem of inequality.

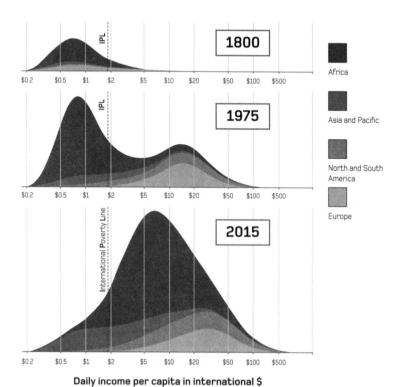

Daily income per capita in international $

The twin peaks on the graph of global income distribution have merged into one as poorer areas of the world have become wealthier.

# Surveillance

In 2013, former CIA operative Edward Snowden revealed how Western governments spy on their own citizens through the Five Eyes security services alliance of US, UK, Canada, Australia and New Zealand. Knowing this hasn't made people more careful. George Orwell's *Nineteen Eighty-Four* vision of ubiquitous surveillance has been embraced and embellished with location trackers and front-facing cameras in phones, and microphones masquerading as speakers in every room of our homes.

In his 1998 non-fiction book *The Transparent Society*, sci-fi author David Brin foresees a future of ubiquitous surveillance – but, rather than the state, it is the general public at the controls of myriad invisible cameras. This 'sousveillance' would see parents always knowing the location of their children and police officers being aware that untold numbers of citizens scrutinize their arrests. Brin doesn't especially like this vision, but sees it as better than the alternative of mass state surveillance. In the best foreseeable future, we all watch the watchers.

# Privacy

Google knows us better than anyone. It tracks our every move and we don't tend to lie when asking questions of a search engine. Privacy as we know it will become a thing of the past, but future humans seem unlikely to care. The trade-off for sacrificing privacy is massive convenience. Social media allows us to present our lives to the world, our information then passed around. Dave Eggers's 2014 book *The Circle* describes a next-generation social media company with slogans 'privacy is theft' and 'secrets are lies' – of course, it is your right not to share your medical records, but you are making the global database weaker by 'stealing' knowledge from your fellow citizens. With so much information about us available, identity theft is the risk. Biometric information, whether fingerprints, face trackers, voice prints, iris scans, under-skin blood flow or even instant DNA tests, defines who we are. In the present this is outsourced and hackable. The blockchain (see page 86) will let us take ownership of our own data, which will be distributed in such a way that no one else can access it, circumventing the need for passwords.

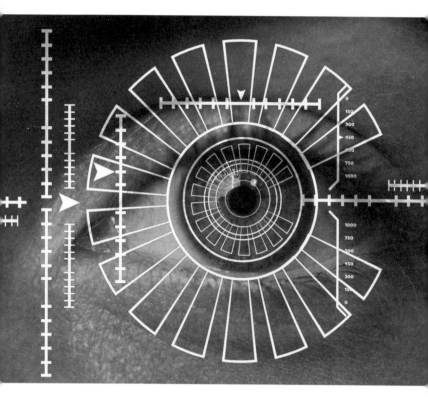

# Precrime

**P**redictive policing shouldn't always need technology – habitual burglars are normally known; school shooters may leave clues. But in 2010 George Mohler and Jeffrey Brantingham, both from UCLA, created an algorithm that predicted hotspots for follow-up crimes, in much the same way that aftershocks are predicted following an earthquake. The technology has been implemented in several US states and UK counties, and is ten times more likely to predict the location of future crime than random beat policing, allowing better allocation of resources. However, algorithms are only as effective as their training data (see page 112) and in 2016 the American Civil Liberties Union complained about racial profiling and a lack of transparency. It is easier to predict trends than individuals, but statistician Richard Berk has been working in Norway to see if he can identify who will turn to crime before the age of 18. As more predictive technology is developed, complete with increased real-time surveillance, individuals will likely be targeted. Knowing someone is likely to commit a crime opens up questions of free will.

# Forecasting crime in Washington DC

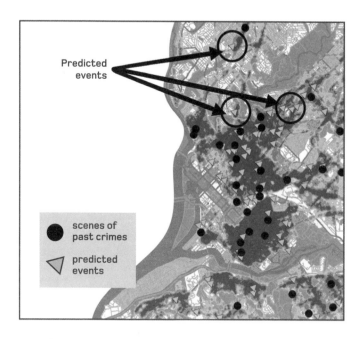

In predicting purse snatchings, forecasters study scenes of past crimes in order to pinpoint the locations of future crimes.

# Law enforcement

Policing requires consent – to engage public trust, near-future forces should have mandatory body cameras, strong public digital presence and transparency of operations. Research also shows that establishing comprehensive DNA databases of criminals reduces reoffending rates by nearly 50%, meaning national and global registers seem inevitable. By 2030, one-quarter of Dubai's police force will be robots. The REEM Dubai police robot is on duty 24/7. Moving on wheels with a humanoid upper body, it uses facial recognition cameras and has a link to a control room, plus a touchscreen for citizens to access services. In contrast, Samsung's SRG-A1 sentry robot guards the Korean demilitarized zone, equipped with cameras and heat and motion sensors, but also machine guns and grenade launchers – not fired autonomously. While future robotic police officers will patrol the streets and the skies, most crime will be digital, involving a technological arms race with cyber criminals or unfriendly governments. Policing this will prove beyond the capabilities of humans, meaning AI will run the operation, integrated into smart-city life (see page 90).

PAL Robotics' REEM Dubai police robot.

# Justice

If accused of a crime, would you rather go before a human or an AI judge? What use a jury of your peers when machine intelligence can weigh the evidence? In 2016, University College London's Nikolaos Aletras developed an AI judge that reached the same conclusion as a human judge in four out of five cases, but it will likely be decades until its successors take charge. However, artificial intelligence is already used in courtrooms with risk-scoring algorithms predicting how likely a guilty party is to reoffend. Although convicted felons are not marked on 'race', the inclusion of such factors as income and where they live has led critics to say there is algorithmic bias (see page 112) against ethnic groups.

Justice goes beyond the courtroom, with humans proving more motivated if things are perceived to be fair. Sharing the benefits of technological progress will be one way for a more just future. Once The Singularity (see page 316) happens, so long as the goals of the superintelligence align with those of humanity, we will likely see an entirely new era of fairness using advanced moral concepts.

# Punishment

**D**espite a general downward trend in crime, the global prison population rose 20% from 2000 to 2015. By 2018, 141 countries had abolished the death penalty with executions declining globally. *Crime and Punishment* author Fyodor Dostoevsky wrote 'The degree of civilization in a society can be judged by entering its prisons.' The official purposes of imprisonment are: punishment; protecting wider society from dangerous offenders; and rehabilitating prisoners. Given the neglected prison systems in many nations, one punishment is likely to be depriving prisoners of access to technology to keep up with progress outside. Philosopher Rebecca Roache has speculated on how punishment might change in the future. For heinous crimes, a 30-year 'life sentence' can seem inadequate so we might adjust how prisoners perceive time, either through virtual reality, pharmaceuticals or even brain uploading (see page 276). This could enable prisoners to serve subjectively lengthy sentences that happen in 24 hours of objective time, with punishments followed by long periods of rehabilitation.

# Religion

A Gallup International survey of 50,000 people in 57 countries revealed the number of those claiming to be religious fell from 77% to 68% between 2005 and 2011. Many nations (Japan, the United Kingdom, South Korea, Germany) that were heavily religious a century ago now report some of the lowest rates of belief. People in these countries have prospered and perhaps no longer require Marx's 'opiate of the masses', suggesting continued global religious decline. America is an outlier in terms of religion versus wealth, but even there atheism is on the rise and faith in decline, albeit from a high base.

Yet The Singularity (see page 316) is imbued with religious imagery, and belief in its desirability has been called 'singularitarianism'. It's even rumoured Silicon Valley figures are funding fringe Singularity religious groups to increase likely human acceptance of AI. Further, if the definition of God is as the creator of the Universe, if we believe we are living in a simulation perhaps we should worship the programmers.

# Animal rights

Despite sharing almost all our DNA, in 2018 New York's Court of Appeal denied chimpanzees Tommy and Kiko rights of habeus corpus brought on their behalves by the Nonhuman Rights Project. Even so, appeals Judge Eugene Fahey agreed the question needed to be addressed and that, 'While it may be arguable that a chimpanzee is not a "person", there is no doubt that it is not merely a thing'. American philosopher Tom Regan's *The Case for Animal Rights* argues complex animals are 'subjects of a life' and this should guarantee a degree of rights. But while we might conceive future gorillas and chimps, whales and dolphins, having rights, what about mice and rats, or cockroaches, or bacteria? Responsibilities often accompany rights, or require the owner to understand the concept, and some argue against animal rights for these reasons, yet babies and young children have rights. Adult humans who are mentally incapacitated for whatever reasons have rights. Future communication with most higher-functioning animals (see page 74) will likely be a game-changer for the status of nonhuman animals in society.

# Robot love

One of the earliest uses for humanoid robots has been for sex (see page 64). Society has always imposed limits on which humans other humans should be allowed to love, but these taboos are changing. Humans have often anthropomorphized machines and this is becoming increasingly so as the machines grow smarter, but at what point might a human and machine enter into a legal loving relationship? In his 2009 *Love and Sex with Robots*, AI expert David Levy suggests sex, relationships and even marriage to robots could be normal by 2050.

One way this may happen is through human enhancement (see page 284) and our merging with technology, which may blur the definitions of 'human' and 'robot' to the point that, in the future, robots will inevitably love and marry other robots. Will entirely mechanical, intelligent robots ever be able to fall in love with unenhanced humans who, to the robots, will be biological machines? Experts are divided, but the prospect is intriguing.

# Robot rights

Fiction has frequently imbued inorganic beings with a desire to become human, from Pinocchio to Star Trek's Mr Data. If an acceptance of animal consciousness requires the granting of some degree of inalienable rights (see page 196), then they must also come for conscious machines, should that happen with The Singularity (see page 316).

An argument against nonhuman animal rights is that they do not have the same level of mental capacity as humans. Once machines have overtaken humans as the most intelligent beings on Earth and the future has passed into their control, the question of their rights becomes a moot point. What then becomes relevant is whether the superintelligent machines acknowledge a small or large level of inalienable rights for humans. Given we hope superintelligences will maintain values in alignment with our own, how we treat animals in the present may be a decisive driver in terms of how future machines decide to treat us.

# Society

Societies come in all shapes and sizes, united through social interaction, geography, culture, and nowadays digital, with online communities straddling national and continental boundaries. History has shown human society cannot be imposed but must evolve organically, as evidenced by the collapse of the Soviet Union. Often, opposition to a common foe has seen societies come together, such as in times of war. In 2016, when Korean Go player Lee Sedol was challenged by Google's AlphaGo AI (see page 116), many humans united behind their champion and against the machine. This phenomenon will rise through the 21st century as society faces disruption, akin to the Luddites in the Industrial Revolution. Space colonization offers great prospects for humans to create new (or try to preserve old) societies of their choosing, with separation and very different physical environments making terrestrial societal norms an irrelevance. If humans succeed in brain uploading (see page 276), dividing society between organic and the new digital humans will be the most profound change in the history of our species.

# Population growth

One billion people lived in 1800 – by 2018 it was 7.7 billion. Depending when you start counting, that's 3–8% of all humans who've ever lived. Projections take it to 9 billion in 2037, 10 billion by 2055 and 11 billion around 2088, but with the rate of growth significantly tailing off. Around 50 billion 'humans' in total lived prior to the first agricultural revolution, in groups of 20 to 50. From 10,000 years ago until the Industrial Revolution saw another 50 billion, mostly in settlements of around 500 to 2,000 people. In our industrial era, around 20 billion have lived, in cities containing roughly 100,000 to 10 million. Economist Robin Hanson describes these as three eras, each hosting populations of the same order of magnitude but the size of communities being roughly the square of the previous one. Each era also encompasses 7–10 doublings of the world's economic capacity to produce valued things – the global economy currently doubles around every 15 years. Admitting these are speculative ideas, the next era would see 'human' communities of 10 billion to 100 trillion – only possible if these are digital humans or ems (see page 292).

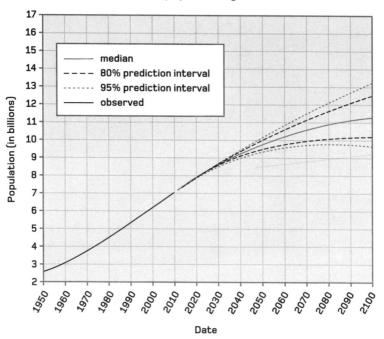

**World population growth**

The projected global population up to 2100
showing 80% and 95% confidence levels.

# Poverty

Global surveys show money buys happiness; low incomes imply poor health and education. The World Bank reports that the number living below its $1.90-a-day definition of extreme poverty more than halved from 1.85 billion in 1990 to 736 million in 2015; its aim, in partnership with the UN's sustainable development goals, is complete eradication of extreme poverty by 2030. Every day more than 200,000 people are lifted out of extreme poverty, yet the 2030 target appears out of reach due to falling economic growth rates, with current estimates projecting 400 million poor by that date. Around 85% of these will be in sub-Saharan Africa with the Gates Foundation suggesting Nigeria and the Democratic Republic of Congo will be home to the majority of all the world's poorest by 2050. The International Monetary Fund suggests five areas that are critical for sustainable and inclusive growth to eradicate poverty: education, health, water and sanitation, roads and electricity. Delivering on this will require significant economic growth, political and climate stability and political will from the rest of humanity to intervene.

# Fertility

In many countries people are living longer and having fewer children. The 'replacement rate' of children per woman in order to maintain a population is approximately 2.1. It's long been clear that wealthier nations have declining birthrates. The 20th century saw replacement rates of 4.5–7, but the global figure in 2017 was around 2.5. German economist Max Roser attributes this to the empowerment of women and the increased well-being and status of children. According to the CIA World Factbook, in 2018 replacement rates varied between 0.83 for Singapore and 6.49 for Niger, with the United Kingdom 1.88 and United States 1.87. Wealth isn't the only factor in the decline. A 2017 study by Israeli epidemiologist Hagai Levine showed Western sperm counts had halved in the 40 preceding years. Suggested factors are stress, obesity and exposure to chemicals and pesticides, with no evidence of decline in South America, Asia or Africa. Research is needed to understand the causes, but parallel improvements in medical technology suggest the future won't be child free.

# World fertility rates 1950 to 2100

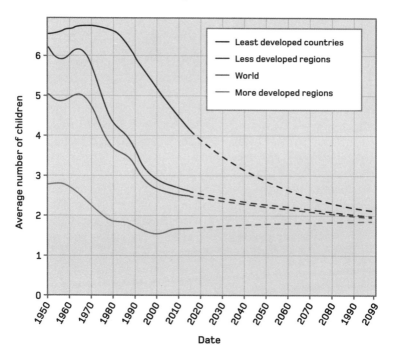

United Nations' actual and projected fertility rates showing
why global population growth is slowing to a halt

# Globalization

Historically our connections extended just a few kilometres, the fastest goods carried on horseback. Today's most important commodity – information – travels at the speed of light. This has led to the rise of mega corporations with global supply chains and mass movement of labour. Increasing globalization appears inevitable. Future nations will have relative wealth proportional to their resources in terms of population and raw materials. Such a situation will see China overtake the United States as the world's richest nation in around 2030. In the West, an antiglobalization movement is attempting to curtail the unfettered power of the multinationals exercised through trade agreements and deregulated financial markets. Economist Joseph Stiglitz suggests globalization is leading to greater inequality with an uber-rich class. He thinks there will be a significant backlash unless a shift in priorities favours social protection without protectionism (taxing imports to deter foreign competition). He believes this will temper the excesses of both capitalism and globalization, to deliver more sustainable growth and higher standards of living for most citizens.

# Mega corporations

Of the world's six most valuable companies in 2018, only Apple (first) and Microsoft (fourth) were over 25 years old, with upstarts Facebook (fifth) and China's Alibaba (sixth) still teenagers. The companies that will dominate the world economy in 2040 may not yet exist. A 2015 World Development Movement report listed the 100 most economically powerful global entities by annual revenue – 31 were nations and 69 corporations. Apple's revenues were bigger than Russia's GDP; in the future it's likely mega corporations will become more important as nations struggle to support citizens in the automated economy. In the West, we choose to be part of the Google, Amazon or Apple ecosystems; in China, Alibaba and Tencent dominate. To be an employee of such a company is highly desirable, but the future will see greater rewards for being a customer, receiving income in exchange for data handed over. To control the power of the mega corporations, international agreements will bring nation states closer together, and only a world government (see page 232) will truly be able to control and tax the corporations – if it can be run successfully.

An aerial photograph of Apple's headquarters, Apple Park, in Cupertino, California.

# Terrorism

The world changed forever in 2001 when al-Qaeda terrorists attacked the World Trade Center and the Pentagon, leading to an enormous escalation of resources invested in the 'War on Terror'. Norwegian historian Brynjar Lia argues that increasing globalization motivates anti-Western sentiments. It fuelled the jihadist ideologies behind the events of 2001 and has provoked subsequent mass-casualty terrorism attacks in Europe and the United States. Lia claims society is sufficiently vulnerable for there to be no let up of opportunity for terrorists to create fear through new modes of attack. Drones and synthetic biology are two avenues likely to be used in spreading fear through future populations. As we approach human-level artificial general intelligence (AGI), unless safety and widespread benefits can be guaranteed, many will feel justified in orchestrating terror to prevent it happening. Into the far future individuals will have the power to send asteroids careering into inhabited planets or to bombard cities with high-energy lasers from space. For humanity to survive, our morality must mature faster than our technology.

The 2001 terrorist attack on New York's World Trade Center.

# Cyber warfare

GCHQ, cyber arm of the security services, is the UK's largest employer of postgraduate mathematicians, actively monitoring global communications. Despite such capabilities, mirrored elsewhere, the networked infrastructure explosion of the early 21st century has not been matched with a similar growth in robust security, making most nations vulnerable to cyber attack. In 2010, international inspectors and technicians at Iran's uranium enrichment facility puzzled over the repeated failure of centrifuges. The computer virus Stuxnet, developed by the NSA, had released pressure valves causing the centrifuges to stop working. The UK's National Cyber Security Centre stated in 2017 that Russian hackers were targeting media, telecoms and energy companies. Chinese tech companies ZTE and Huawei have products banned in several Western countries for fear of compromising vital infrastructure. If an enemy could infiltrate battlefield weapons to prevent them working, wars would be over quickly, but securing satellites, power grids, transport systems, food and water supplies is as important as military technology. Future cyber warfare will simply be warfare.

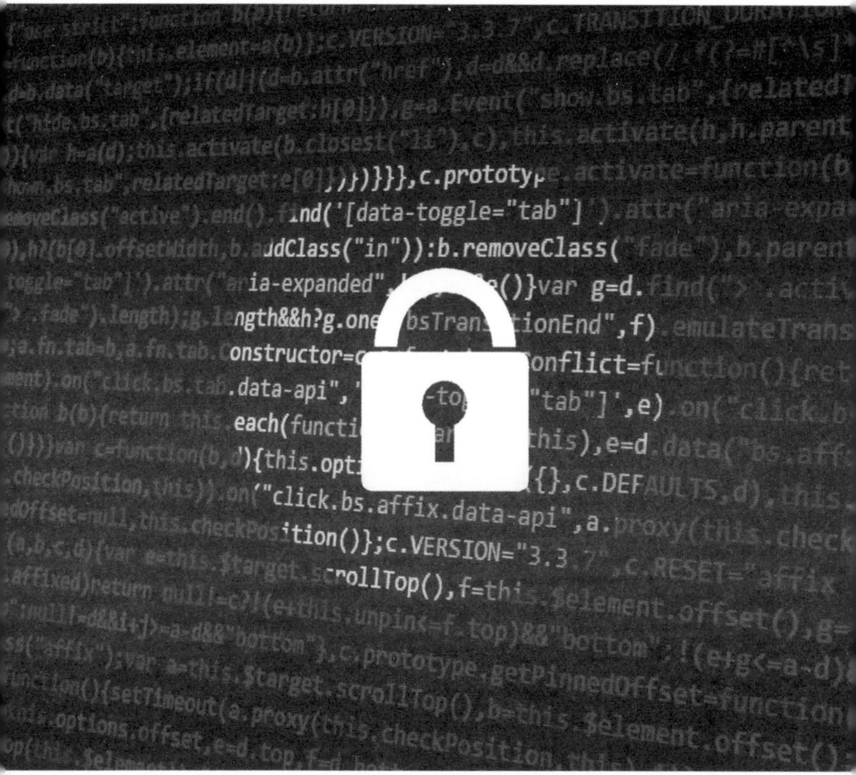

# Drone warfare

**D**rones are popular among politicians for removing humans from the 'theatre of war'. In his first year as president, Barack Obama oversaw more drone strikes than there were during the whole of the preceding Bush era. Currently, military drones do not have full autonomy, but require a 'human in the loop' to make life or death decisions, although quite what that means is open to question. With proliferation to many other nations and also terror groups, certainly by 2030 and probably sooner, can we be safe from airborne threats? While it remains possible to stop one, two or a handful of drones, the US Department of Defense has also been developing micro drone swarms such as Perdix. The future will see swarms of hundreds, thousands and eventually millions of hypersonic drones designed to overpower defences and deliver their payloads. No human will be capable of defending themselves against such a barrage. Aware of the threat, a coalition of thinkers and technology leaders has signed a global pledge to ban autonomous weapons. How the future unfolds will be defined by whether this is acted upon.

# Totalitarianism

Totalitarianism is a centralized form of government that requires subservience to the state. Historically, such regimes have struggled to prevent information from the outside world filtering through. Future technology may work the other way, helping to secure totalitarianism by manipulating information available to the population, including the use of 'deep fakes' of trusted figures to utter whatever pronouncements the state wishes. One of the fears of those studying existential risk is not simply that there will be totalitarian forms of government, but that technology will enable the possibility of a global totalitarian regime that will stunt humanity's potential. By continually monitoring the entire population, censoring information deemed hazardous, or altering the brain chemistry of citizens to make them content to be governed in this way, humans and/or superintelligence could secure power forever. But if we can create colonies away from Earth (see pages 346–9) then any form of centralized control becomes more difficult as interactions are limited by the speed of light.

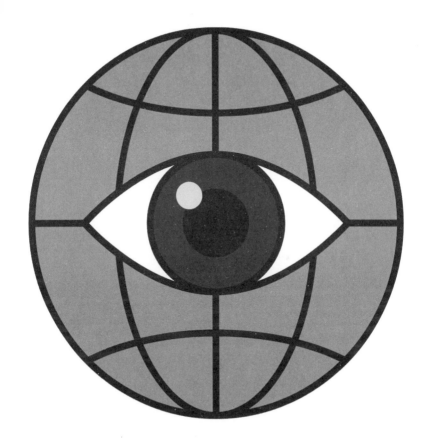

# Democracy

Many new democracies emerged following the collapse of the Soviet Union in 1991. But between 2000 and 2015 democracy retreated in 27 nations, leading Stanford University's Larry Diamond to suggest we've entered a 'democratic recession'. India will become the world's most populous nation in 2022. Whether democracy triumphs may depend on India overhauling China as the number one economic superpower, which would make it politically influential, too. While India is set to overtake Japan by 2040, overtaking China and the US depends on as yet unknown technological breakthroughs.

Should we invent machines with superior AGI, could they not run countries better than elected politicians? If humans could still vote, might choices be between the different values of the AGIs? And if brain uploading (see page 276) is successful, with the subsequent explosion in the number of (digital) humans, are all their votes to count equally – especially if many are in the same clans (see page 294) descended from a small number of individuals?

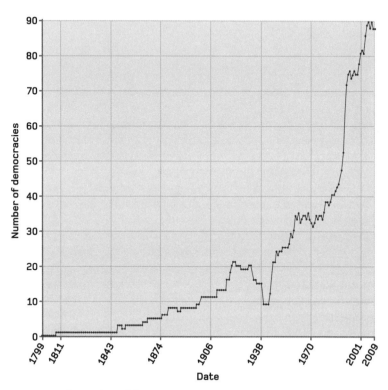

The number of democratic countries during the last 200 years.

# Direct government

People vote on a daily basis on who should win TV talent contests yet only elect governments every few years. We can express preferences on most things from the comfort of our sofas, but elections require physical journeys to outdated polling stations or cumbersome postal-voting practices. If government is to be by the people for the people, it is due an upgrade.

Switzerland is the most prominent direct democracy, where citizens vote on major policy issues up to four times a year with the dates of these polls fixed until 2034. The country is cited as a model of direct government going into the future. For any vote reforming the constitution to succeed, it needs a majority of both the voters and the 26 electoral districts (cantons). Any citizen can propose a vote that needs sufficient support within a fixed timeframe, such as that on universal basic income in 2016 (see page 44). An obvious issue is the risk of voters approving contradictory or potentially damaging policies, but this can be overcome with an engaged, informed and educated electorate.

## DIRECT

Government

## REPRESENTATIVE

Government

The law

The law

Elected
representative

Vote

Vote

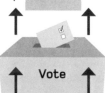

THE PEOPLE

THE PEOPLE

# Prediction markets

How should an electorate evaluate the impact of conflicting policies proposed by their politicians and the way these are portrayed by a ratings-hungry media? Prediction markets are betting tools for providing unbiased information in order to help people make better decisions. Companies have used them to determine which drugs were likely to succeed in chemical trials or to predict when products would be ready for launch. A 'futarchy' is democracy evolved to incorporate prediction markets, proposed by economist Robin Hanson in his influential paper 'Shall we vote on values, but bet on beliefs?' A 2040 proposal might be to spend 40 billion euros to build a road bridge between Spain and Morocco on the basis it will increase GDP by 2050. The prediction market offers shares of equal value on the anticipated GDP in a decade, based on whether or not the project was funded. These are exchanged in a marketplace – the market with the greatest expected outcome becomes policy, with shares in the losing market refunded. Come 2050, those who participated in the winning market will gain or lose depending on the accuracy of their predictions.

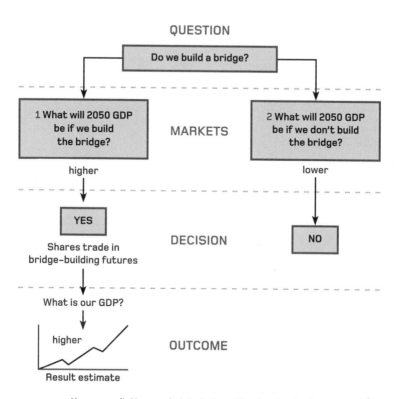

How a prediction market is designed to decide whether
or not to embark on a major infrastructure project.

# World peace

Examining male death rates per head of population in England, despite two world wars, the 20th century was the most peaceful since the 11th century. The second half of the 20th century was the most peaceful in Europe's history; the number of conflicts globally has increased, but related casualties have plummeted. Is this promising downward trend the result of nuclear deterrence or are we simply delaying a larger future conflict? Given the potential use of AI in future wars, and the nuclear winter that would result from any major nuclear conflict, there is the prospect that the next war will be humanity's last. International tensions will arise from technological inequality between countries, overpopulation, the impact of climate change – or geoengineering attempts to prevent it. However, cognitive scientist Steven Pinker believes the overall decrease in lives lost due to conflicts shows the institution of war is seeing its demise, and can be eliminated through our post-Enlightenment desire for human flourishing. If he is right, future humans may look on world peace as the crowning achievement of humanity.

# The end of money

Cowrie shells were perhaps the first currency a few thousand years ago. Minted coins followed, then notes, but in the 21st century cash is on the retreat. In the UK, in 2006, 62% of payments were made in cash. A decade later that was 40%. By 2026 it will be 21%. But this decline in cash, mirrored around the world, doesn't yet mean an end to money. There are bank transfers, debit and credit cards, Android and Apple Pay, Paypal, and myriad other ways of transferring an amount of money from one party to another. Until 2009 governments created currency, but Bitcoin (see page 46) began a shift in power. As part of the rise of mega corporations, it's likely these will develop their own currencies too. However, money is only necessary if society has scarcity – much of the digital economy is already 'free' because scarcity doesn't exist with digital products. Step changes in economic growth or entering an era of radical abundance (see page 372) will see this happen with physical products too, likely rendering money unnecessary in all its forms. In the *Star Trek* post-scarcity utopia, this happens around the end of the 22nd century.

# World government

The League of Nations was founded in 1920 to ensure global conflict wasn't repeated following WWI. After WWII it was replaced by the United Nations and its enforcement arm, the Security Council. The globalization of trade saw common economic interest spread through several international institutions, but the different political systems of East and West make a further coming together difficult. That didn't stop German political scientist Alexander Wendt penning the paper 'Why a world state is inevitable'. Wendt expects a world government 'within 100 to 200 years'. International lawyer Anne-Marie Slaughter dismisses such a view but argues in her book *A New World Order* that, in some ways, we are already overseen by a complex network of transnational bodies. Pressure for global governance will come from: otherwise untaxable global mega corporations; climate change; fear of conflict with autonomous weaponry; or even the discovery of intelligent extraterrestrials (see page 362). If superintelligences are created, these would likely converge into a single global power that would govern the planet.

LEAGUE OF NATIONS

SOCIÉTÉ DES NATIONS

# Independence

No previous government has had the capacity to oversee the whole planet, yet those tools are now, or will become, available through the 21st century. It means world government would be possible and, perhaps, the only way to solve some of humanity's problems, such as climate change. But if we spread as we need to beyond Earth (see page 334), then the constraints of the laws of nature will make centralized rule of our species impossible, with independence or autonomy inevitable. The limiting factor is the speed of light. It takes 1.3s for a signal from Earth to reach the Moon and vice versa. That may not sound much, but in an ultra-high-speed future, it puts even Earth's governance of a lunar colony in doubt. Further out, communication with Mars would vary from 4 to 24 minutes; reaching the outer solar system would run into several hours. If worldships (see page 358) ever take humans to the nearest known worlds beyond the solar system, Proxima Centauri B and Alpha Centauri B, the colonies there might declare independence and it would take four years for Earth to find out.

# How we'll stay healthy

However more wealthy individuals or societies are in future, if we cannot live healthy lives, the point is lost. Global studies show health outcomes correlate with healthcare investments, indicating we understand the basics of physical health and can make steady progress in the future. Specific initiatives include a World Health Organization (WHO) framework to eliminate malaria in at least 35 countries by 2030.

As the world changes, the 'healthy mind, healthy body' adage has rarely seemed more appropriate. Jack Ma, founder of Chinese tech giant Alibaba, says that today's customers are showing an increasing preference for participating in activities that promote their well-being – and sharing those experiences with their friends. The early decades of the 21st century have seen steep rises in mental illness, which traditionally has received less resource than physical health. The WHO anticipates depression will be the largest single healthcare burden by 2030, costing the global economy $6 trillion.

Promoting mental health and well-being is among the UN's 2030 Sustainable Development Goals.

# Antibiotics

Penicillin, the first known antibiotic, has saved 200 million lives. Although new drugs and mechanisms have been devised since its discovery by Alexander Fleming in 1928, the uncontrolled use of penicillin and other antibiotics has led to the evolution and spread of antimicrobial-resistant (AMR) bacteria, now common across the globe. Without work on new antibiotics, by 2050 global annual AMR-related deaths will rise from 700,000 to 10 million as superbugs increase. In 2015, teixobactin became the first new potential antibiotic for a decade, created using a new bacteria-culturing technology called iChip – while almost all microbes die in laboratories and can't be assessed for new medicines, this 'isolation chip' allows them to be studied in situ in soil. Even if trials go smoothly, it won't reach the market until 2025. Without effective antibiotics, common surgical procedures such as appendectomies and caesarean sections could become life-threatening. Yet the global market for patented antibiotics in 2016 was worth $4.7 bn, the same as a single cancer drug. Technology offers promise, but more must be done to incentivize pharmaceutical companies.

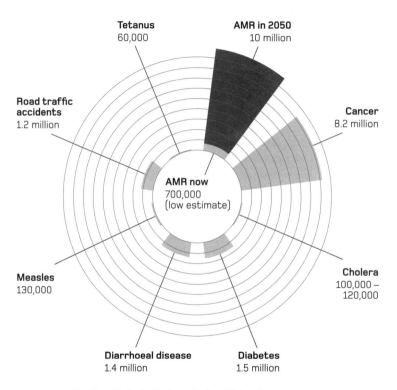

Deaths attributable to antimicrobial resistance every year compared to some other major causes of death.

# Obesity

The WHO reports global obesity trebled between 1975 and 2016. Almost two billion adults were overweight (of whom one-third were obese) with 38% of Americans and 27% of Britains obese. By 2022, there will be more obese than underweight children and adolescents. By 2045 half the UK adult population and 55% of Americans will be obese.

Obesity through perceived weight discrimination or 'weight stigma' is associated with body dissatisfaction, depression, anxiety, bulimia and low self-esteem. As well as needing to eat less and exercise more, heredity factors play a major role. Beyond that, scientific opinion remains divided as to the causes and solutions. As well as increasing portion sizes, diets high in sugars appear to promote obesity which led to the UK government introducing a 'sugar tax' on soft drinks in 2018. Type 2 diabetes and coronary heart disease are two of the medical time bombs lying in wait and it may even be that we start to see a life expectancy decline (see page 268).

# Stem cells

Stem cells have the remarkable ability to divide into copies of themselves or any other of the body's 200 or so specialized cell types (pluripotency). In 1998, developmental biologist James Thomson derived the first human embryonic stem cell line. Then, in 2007 Kyoto University's Shinya Yamanaka discovered how to induce pluripotency in adult human cells. As well as growing replacement organs (see page 272), early treatments will come for macular degeneration, spinal cord injuries and diabetes.

So far, only around 10 fully functioning human cell types have been created, such as dopamine-producing neurons to treat Parkinson's disease. More diversity is the challenge for future treatments, but it took Israeli scientists 15 years to coax embryonic stem cells into pancreatic cells to produce insulin. Development costs are also high, but as they fall, one future use will be to reduce the amount of medical animal testing through disease-in-a-dish studies in which scientists test treatments directly.

# Proposed regeneration of an entire tooth using stem cells

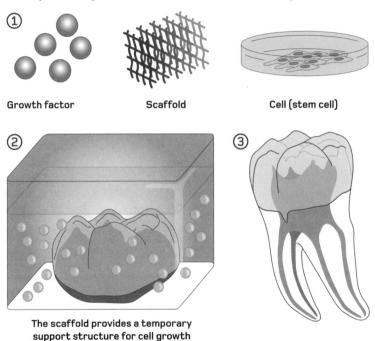

① Growth factor    Scaffold    Cell (stem cell)

② The scaffold provides a temporary support structure for cell growth

③

Growth factors would be added to a scaffold containing dental stem cells enabling a new tooth to grow that can be transplanted into the patient.

# Genomics

The Human Genome Project, which ran from 1990–2003 promised a new era of medicine and understanding, as the genetic make-up of humans was finally revealed. But genetics, the study of individual genes and their role in inheritance, showed that only a handful of medical conditions arise from single-gene disorders. Genomics is the study of the genome – the whole set of genes in a cell – and the complex interactions between different genes. It seeks to unlock causes of, and treatments for, human disease and to reveal how different genetic traits arise.

Given the differences between individuals, identifying general patterns requires us to look at a wide cross-section of humans. The United Kingdom's 100,000 Genomes Project completed sequencing in 2018 and has an initial focus on rare diseases, cancer (both strongly linked to changes in the genome) and infectious diseases. Whatever transpires, genomics is expected to lead to more precise diagnosis, faster clinical trials and new cures taking effect by 2030.

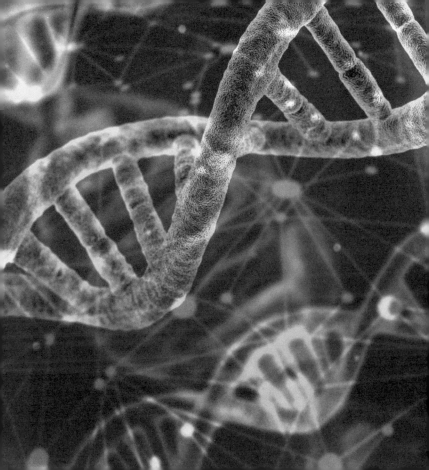

# Personalized medicine

Between 2003 and 2016 the cost of sequencing an individual genome fell to $1000 and is projected to reach $1 by 2025; the availability of data from individual sensor technology (see page 244) is also set to skyrocket. Not every drug or treatment works for every patient, so the goal of personalized medicine is to combine both technologies to introduce individual treatments for disease – realizing the vision of genetics pioneer Larry Hood's 'P4-medicine' in making it predictive, personalized, preventative and participatory. Already we can test if patients with Type 1 diabetes injecting insulin would do better on simple tablets, or whether breast cancer tests positive for a particular protein (HER2) and is therefore treatable using Herceptin. Scientists are continually researching such 'biomarkers' to tell which patients will be susceptible to a particular disease or responsive to a certain treatment. Central to the success of personalized medicine is the collection and analysis of medical data from billions of humans, which raises questions over current business models for health insurance and other societal ideas about privacy (see page 184).

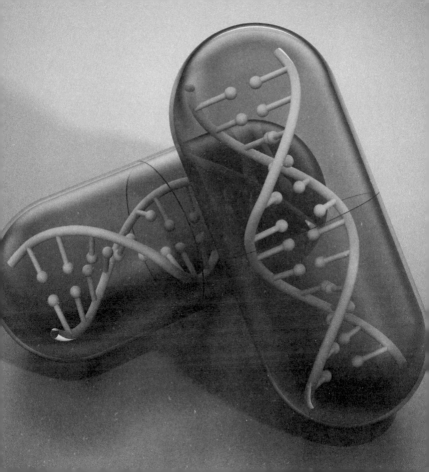

# Gene editing

In 2012, scientists from the Howard Hughes Medical Institute published the discovery of CRISPR Cas9 gene editing. Cas9 is an enzyme associated with the CRISPR (Clustered Regularly Interspaced Short Palindromic Repeats) array, which occurs naturally in bacteria. It makes cuts in DNA to improve a bacterium's immune system. The paper demonstrated how to use Cas9 to direct it to cut anywhere in a genome, replacing a piece of DNA that causes disease with a healthy strand. It has great agricultural potential and in humans will be used for DNA substitutions in genetic diseases and chronic ailments. In 2018, medical ethicists were shocked when Chinese scientist He Jiankui announced the birth of twins whose genome had been edited to increase HIV resistance. This came without significant experimentation on nonhuman primates to determine risks. The very first trials in adult humans will happen shortly, seeing treatments onstream in the 2030s. The far future promises genetically engineered human babies free from many diseases with great intelligence and athleticism built into their genomes.

With climate change threatening that the world's supply of cacao will be severely depleted by 2050, the Mars chocolate company is currently working with Berkeley's Innovative Genomics Institute to genetically modify cacao pods to survive on less water and at higher temperatures, preventing a chocapocalypse.

# Robot carers

As people are living longer and birthrates are declining, the age profile of the population is rising. Who will look after the elderly and infirm? People enjoy living in their own homes and having a degree of independence, but many need help getting out of bed, bathing, preparing meals and cleaning. By 2025, with a projected deficit of 370,000 carers for its ageing population, the Japanese government proposes a Robot Strategy that will provide robotic support to four out of five care recipients. To Western eyes the lack of human contact and companionship may seem shocking, but Japanese culture is far more accepting of robots. As they become more prominent in the West, the transition to a society full of robot carers there seems inevitable, too.

Further ahead, tactile robot animals will offer companionship to their owners, while robot chefs prepare nutritious meals, having determined the needs of the human based on Internet of things data (see page 80).

The Care-O-bot® from Fraunhofer IPA is on hand to provide everything from entertainment and refreshments to communication with others and emergency support.

# Robotic surgery

Would you like to be operated on by a surgeon who never gets tired or distracted, who has learned from every example of the procedure you're about to undertake and is superior to the world's top surgeons? But who happens to be a robot? A halfway house is the da Vinci Surgical System with four robotic arms ending in double-jointed wrists that control various instruments. It is designed to facilitate minimally invasive complex surgery, but controlled by a surgeon at a console. As of 2017, over 4,000 units were operating worldwide. The Virtual Incision robot is aiming for FDA approval to perform operations from inside the body, residing in the abdominal cavity, while the first fully autonomous robotic surgeons include the Smart Tissue Autonomous Robot that has outperformed human surgeons in several tests. New robots will perform long-distance telesurgery, some even tested in zero gravity to prepare for future operations in space. Even further ahead, deep-learning techniques will allow autonomous robotic surgeons to learn entirely new techniques in a few hours and perform operations with superhuman precision.

A surgical room in a hospital, with robotic technology equipment.

# Tricorders

New technology often emulates science fiction and nowhere is this more apparent than with the realization of a 'Star Trek tricorder' – a portable device packed with sensors designed to diagnose multiple conditions. To drive the innovation necessary and empower personal healthcare the XPrize Foundation offered a $10m Tricorder Prize to 'develop innovative technologies capable of accurately diagnosing a set of 13 medical conditions independent of a healthcare professional or facility'. It awarded first place to Pennsylvania's Basil Leaf for its DxtER device, which could diagnose and monitor conditions such as diabetes, atrial fibrillation, urinary tract infection, sleep apnoea, stroke, tuberculosis and pneumonia. It is expected to be developed into a consumer product in the 2020s. This means that, in the future, everyone will have instant, low-cost access to high-quality medical analysis, much of it through continuous monitoring. The results will automatically upload to healthcare providers who can intervene at the first sign of anything untoward, bringing enormous efficiency savings to the spiralling costs of medical care.

The Basil Leaf DxtER™ device.

# Exoskeletons

In 2018, Japanese Cyberdyne gained FDA approval for medical use of its HAL (hybrid assisted limb) lower-body exoskeleton – a battery-powered, brain-controlled walking robot that straps to the legs to enhance strength and stability. By using brain commands, the claim is that new neural pathways will develop, enabling patients to walk again after injury. Ford Motor Company began testing upper-body exoskeletons on their assembly lines in 2011, aiming for greater productivity with less energy expended.

Exoskeletons bring many benefits but haven't become mainstream because they are uncomfortable to wear for long periods. The Harvard Biodesign Lab is developing lightweight soft exosuits using innovative textiles and that do not require power supplies. These will continue to become more effective and less obtrusive, until in a few decades they'll become a sensor-laden second skin providing additional strength while connecting us to the Internet of humans (see page 124).

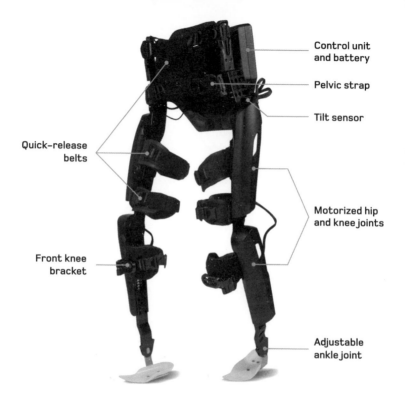

**Control unit and battery**

**Pelvic strap**

**Tilt sensor**

**Quick-release belts**

**Motorized hip and knee joints**

**Front knee bracket**

**Adjustable ankle joint**

ReWalk Robotics have developed a wearable robotic exoskeleton that provides powered hip and knee motion to enable individuals with spinal cord injury to stand upright, walk, turn and climb and descend stairs.

# Artificial wombs

The 'bottling rooms' of Aldous Huxley's *Brave New World* introduced us to ectogenesis – the development of embryos outside the womb. In 2017, science fiction approached science fact when Alan Flake and his team from the Children's Hospital of Philadelphia successfully housed lambs in artificial wombs, keeping six-month-old foetuses alive for four more weeks before removing them from the 'ziplock-like' devices and transitioning to ventilators. This work hopes to give premature human babies further time in a womb-like environment. A year earlier, Magdalena Zernicka-Goetz's Cambridge team matured human embryos for two weeks within chemical mixtures designed to replicate the early womb. Given both initial and final conditions of pregnancy can now be replicated, ectogenesis may not be far away. Future women will be able to choose to have children but not be pregnant, while a foetus within a controlled environment may be safer. This will also provide a straightforward mechanism for all-male couples to have children, and for future children to be born as the product of the genetic material of many humans with no specific mother.

# Human cloning

On 5th July 1996, Dolly the Sheep was born at Edinburgh's Roslin Institute, the first large mammal to be cloned. Dogs, cats and pigs soon followed, but primates proved harder and it wasn't until 2017 that Chinese biologists Sun Qiang and Liu Zhen cloned a pair of macaque monkeys in a major step forward. Genetically identical test subjects remove a major variable in experimental trials. Using gene-editing techniques to create human forms of the conditions, the Chinese researchers want to clone identical monkeys to study Alzheimer's while others are keen to embark on Parkinson's disease research this way. Increased primate experimentation raises ethical questions. The technique also leaves many failed clones along the way – in the case of the macaques, only two were born despite implanting 79 embryos in 21 surrogates. While many countries have laws prohibiting human cloning on ethical grounds, there no longer appear to be any technical barriers. This makes it likely that a scientist and/or rich benefactor will likely achieve this milestone, perhaps in secret, during the 2020s.

# Cancer

Every sixth death in the world is due to cancer, a class of different diseases characterized by out-of-control cell growth that primarily affects the elderly. By stretching life expectancy into the 80s, rates have increased – 12% of the UK population is over 70, but they account for more than half of cancer cases. However, age-corrected death rates for cancer fell 15–20% between 1990 and 2018, the biggest improvements coming in stomach, oesophageal and cervical cancers.

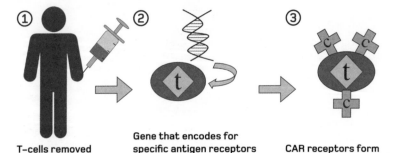

① T-cells removed from patient's blood.

② Gene that encodes for specific antigen receptors incorporated into T-cells.

③ CAR receptors form on cells' surfaces.

Immunotherapy treatments, boosting the body's own defences, look extremely promising – especially CAR (chimeric antigen receptor) T-cell therapy in which white blood cells are removed from a patient, modified to attack malignant cells and reinserted into the body in an example of personalized medicine (see page 246). This approach may eventually work on around 80% of cancers, but is unlikely to become mainstream until 2030. Silicon Valley is also stepping up, assigning supercomputers and cutting-edge AI techniques to better understand the mechanics of cancer. While we'll continue to cure specific cancers, oncologist Barrie Bode says a single 'cure for cancer' won't happen in the next 100 years.

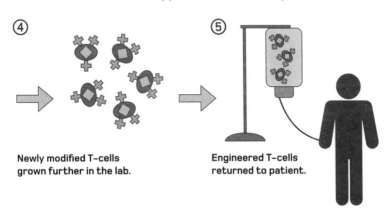

④ Newly modified T-cells
grown further in the lab.

⑤ Engineered T-cells
returned to patient.

# Nanobots

In 2018 Chinese scientists were able to inject nanobots (microscopic robots) made from folded sheets of DNA into mice. They delivered blood-clotting drugs into the blood vessels surrounding tumours, cutting off the blood supply to the cancer. A red blood cell is 7,000nm (0.007mm) wide; a strand of DNA 2nm across. The human vascular system is a 100,000km (60,000 mile) long 3D microfluidic network that allows swimming bots to reach anywhere in the body, but they need a propulsion system. Different research approaches have used biological (based on flagella of bacteria) or synthetic motors to move around, and over the coming decades nanobots will be injected into patients to target a specific site, manipulate diseased or damaged tissues using nano-instruments (either autonomously or guided by a surgeon) and then harmlessly biodegrade. Ever-reducing scale will be a key factor, ultimately enabling the human body to undergo continual renewal at atomic levels using machines based on Eric Drexler's universal assemblers (see page 372).

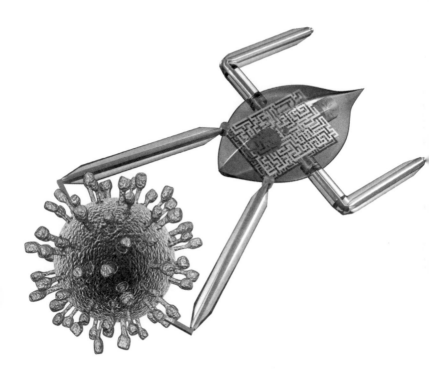

# The quest for immortality

The jellyfish *Turritopsis dohrnii* is biologically immortal. Lab experiments reveal it can reverse ageing and repeatedly return from maturity to its initial lifecycle stage. Humans are some way off, the oldest known being Jeanne Calment, born in Arles, France, in 1875 and dying 122 years later. However, beyond age 105 our risk of dying each year stops increasing, levelling out at 47%. Scientists studying life extension have found calorie-restricted diets to be important – mice can live to the equivalent of 200 human years if they eat less. Human studies discovered a select group of Indiana Amish who have a gene that extends life by around 10%. Among the megarich of Silicon Valley, ending ageing is big business. Following promising research connecting the circulatory systems of old and young mice, Monterey startup Ambrosia conducted anonymous human trials where the rich paid a reported $8,000 to have teenage blood pumped through their veins. More conventionally, Google's parent Alphabet has created a science startup Calico, with an interdisciplinary mission to investigate and extend human lifespan.

*The Fountain of Youth* (1546) by Lucas Cranach the Elder.

# Life-expectancy trends

Until the Industrial Revolution, life expectancy hovered below 40 years. It's now double that in developed countries, while everywhere has life expectancy higher than the very highest value in 1800. Survival rates for older cohorts show this is about more than improving infant mortality. Historically, researchers have queued up to specify a maximum average life expectancy (65 in the 1920s; 85 in the 1990s), but these figures have been exceeded and the graphs continue to rise linearly, suggesting any true maximum lies far off. For 160 years, whichever country topped the charts for female life expectancy has seen a consistent increase of three months per year. For men the rise is equally consistent, but slightly less, widening the gender differential.

Those wanting to live forever hope to surf a wave of longevity to when life expectancy rises by more than one year per year. To achieve that will likely require a revolutionary breakthrough, but just getting close will see ever more improvements in the human condition until immortality is close to being achieved.

# Share of persons surviving to successive ages for persons born 1851 to 2031, England and Wales

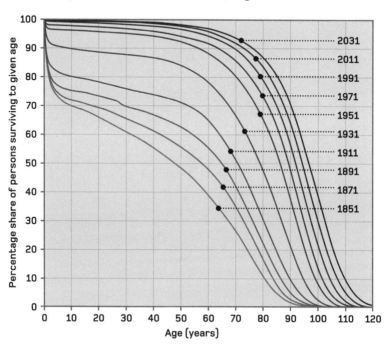

By 2031, 40% of people will live to age 100, double the number four decades earlier as cohorts live longer.

# Engineering negligible senescence

Senescence makes us old. It's what happens when cells have lost the ability to divide further but remain in the body. In 2005, Cambridge engineer Aubrey de Grey proposed this could be thought of as an engineering rather than purely medical problem, co-founding both the SENS (strategies for engineering negligible senescence) and the Methuselah Foundations. While the ultimate hope is to cure and then reverse ageing, a testable near-term goal is to 'make 90 the new 50 by 2030'. Among the strategies are: clearing cells and organs of harmful by-products that build up over time; restoring the function of the circulatory system to youthful levels; measuring DNA and RNA degradation and then restoring it; and increasing the number of youthful stem cells the body has access to. The contention is that the science already exists to make most of this possible, but needs to be applied to the specific problem of ageing. Accepting death as somehow inevitable and failing until recently to begin to address ageing as a disease to be cured is an aspect of our era likely to appal future humans.

# Organ regrowth

A large-scale switch to autonomous vehicles will lead to a dramatic decline in transplantable organs due to the fall in road-traffic deaths. Future technology should instead allow us to receive replacements with our own organs, also eliminating the problem of the body rejecting foreign transplants.

Given Shinya Yamanaka's creation of induced pluripotent stem cells (page 242) we have the building blocks. Joan Nichols at the University of Texas has used them to grow pig lungs in the lab and transplant them successfully into donor animals. At King's College London, Tamir Rashid suggests growing organs inside sheep before transplantation into a human – a concept that might see future hospitals maintaining herds of animals on standby. A technology that could bypass the need for animal intermediaries altogether would be to 3D-print human organs. Prellis Biologics has demonstrated speedy holographic printing of capillaries, a crucial target for future bottom-up tissue engineering and regenerative medicine.

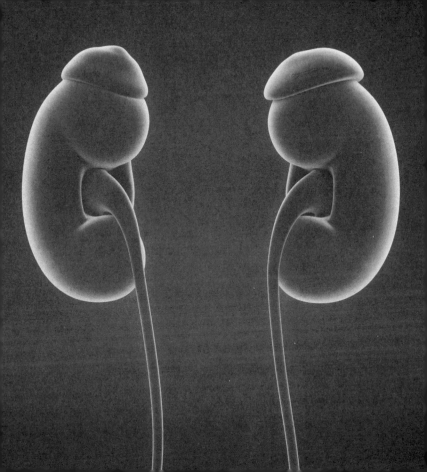

# Cryogenic freezing

In Scottsdale, Arizona, one hundred dead people hang upside down in vats of liquid nitrogen. This is the home of Alcor Life Extension Foundation, first of several companies to offer 'cryonics' – a process by which antifreeze-like cryoprotectants replace bodily fluids as soon after death as possible, before extreme cooling. While we currently use low temperatures to preserve embryos and tissue, science is far from preserving organs this way (for future transplantation, for example). However, the argument by advocates of cryonics is that future tech will be so advanced that, decades or centuries hence, revival may be possible. A cheaper option is to have only your head preserved. The idea is that if future science can revive cryogenically preserved humans, it will also be able to regrow new bodies. Another school of thought suggests that most future humans will be emulated brains living in virtual worlds. An easier route to future immortality may, therefore, be to have cryopreserved brains scanned and uploaded into a future computer (see page 276).

This 'Bigfoot' Dewar is custom-designed to contain four wholebody patients and five neuropatients immersed in liquid nitrogen at –196° Celsius.

# Brain uploading

What if you could use imaging technology to produce an incredibly detailed three-dimensional scan of the human brain; translate the scan into a model of the brain's constituent elements; and reproduce neurocomputational steps using models of the different types of neurons on a sufficiently powerful computer? This method of uploading or brain emulation wouldn't even require us to know exactly how the brain works. Swedes Anders Sandberg and Nick Bostrom have produced a roadmap for how this might happen over decades or centuries, starting simply at first with something like a roundworm, then an invertebrate. Next would likely be different mammals and, once technology becomes more robust, a human. Initially the scans are likely to be destructive making the upload a one-way journey that has to be got right. As technology progresses and scans become passive, it would become possible to back up your 'mind state' on a regular basis, to be able to restore it should anything bad (such as death) happen to you in the interim, making you effectively immortal.

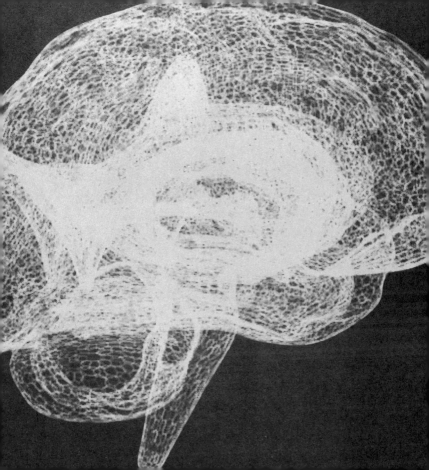

# Posthumans and transhumanism

The genus *Homo* began walking the Earth a few million years ago, with modern humans, *Homo sapiens*, around for the last 200,000 to 300,000. Since the scientific revolution we have learned about survival of the fittest and wonder what's next. Evolution is a continuous process – studying developments in the genome, Stanford's Jonathan Pritchard has shown that, since Roman times, white Britons have become fairer, taller and better able to digest milk. Oxford transhumanist Nick Bostrom defines transhumanism as a way of thinking that proposes to improve the human condition in a transcendent future that begins over the next few decades. He sees humans taking control of evolution in order to create 'posthumans' (without precluding the continued existence of traditional humans). Goals are to significantly extend human lifespans and to physically augment or genetically alter our bodies. Posthumans may be altered to reach great intellectual heights or to become impervious to disease; they may also even be entirely synthetic, while retaining the essence of what it means to be human.

The philosopher Nick Bostrom is known for his work on existential risk, the anthropic principle, human enhancement ethics and superintelligence risks.

# Embryo screening and selection

Few argue with embryo screening for genetic diseases – rates of infantile Tay-Sachs disease (fatal in early childhood) have fallen by 90% in at-risk populations – but should parents be able to choose a child's sex? What about requesting blue eyes? Advances in embryo cell analysis make these possible now, but not yet commonplace. In the next few years we will be able to select more intelligent embryos. Should this become widespread, it will likely take 50 years before the effects begin to manifest, given the more intelligent infants must become adults and then have more intelligent children of their own.

A promising technology to speed things up uses stem-cell-derived gametes to compress the cycle of multiple generations into just one. By deriving sperm and eggs from more intelligent embryonic stem cells, a process of iterated embryo selection would become possible, leading to a potential intelligence arms race around the world as nations compete to birth future intellectual giants to drive economic progress.

Injecting sperm into an egg cell to begin in-vitro fertilization.

# Resurrection

**E**fforts to defy death will likely begin with the resurrection of much-loved pets in mixed reality. You'll still take Fido for a walk, but you'll be the only person to see him. This will soon move on to humans.

In 2016, knowing his father was dying from cancer, James Vlahos recorded him talking about his life and created DadBot, a chatbot that conversed through text messages. Thirty million Facebook users died in the first eight years of its existence and the numbers are rising so that, if still around in 2065 the dead will outnumber the living on the site. This data could be used to create AI versions of the deceased, perhaps sanitized by learning only from what people revealed through social media. If unsatisfied by digital renditions, eventually new physical (perhaps robotic) bodies could be created to house these electronic entities. Once brain uploading becomes possible (projections vary between 2050 and 2400), we can all cheat death by backing up our mind states to be resurrected as often as desired.

# Human enhancement

The first eyeglasses were manufactured in Pisa, Italy, around 1290. Medical enhancements have come a long way, including artificial limbs, eyes and ears that even attempt to rebuild neural pathways, while surgeons use brain implants to bypass damaged areas. Human enhancement isn't solely for treating illness or disability – it will increasingly be used for improving abilities or creating new ones. Adventurers could be given a magnetic sense to always know north when in the wilderness. It might also be desirable to develop our own sonar and radar, using echolocation and radio waves, to give a more accurate map of our place in the world.

Astronomer Royal Martin Rees believes enhancement will completely transform humanity in the far future. He argues it is the destiny of any intelligent spacefaring species to take on so much technology that they become artificial life forms, with vastly enhanced abilities and without the problems from cosmic rays or lack of gravity that space travel presents to organic bodies.

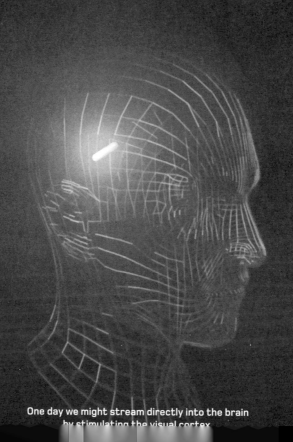

One day we might stream directly into the brain
by stimulating the visual cortex

# Mind expansion

The human brain is the most complex information-processing system we've encountered. Although we don't yet fully understand it, we're taking steps to make it more efficient. The most common stimulant is caffeine, but many academics are turning to modafinil. It does the same job, but has also been shown to boost higher-order cognitive function with few side effects. For those wary of drug-taking, meditation techniques such as mindfulness will rise in popularity, given the benefits shown in brain scans. There's more to mind expansion than brain chemistry, however. American neuroscientist Theodore Berger is currently developing brain implants to help store long-term memories, particularly for Alzheimer's or stroke victims, but with potential to give all of us improved memories. Another route that transhumanists are taking is to recognize and try to overcome our own biases, and to think more rationally. Websites such as 'Less Wrong' and 'Overcoming Bias' demonstrate how challenging rational thinking can be to the status quo, spawning new movements such as effective altruism.

# Mind melds

The ways in which we interact with computers has changed from the punch cards of the 1950s to keyboards, touchscreens and, most recently, voice. In 2017, SpaceX and Tesla's Elon Musk founded Neuralink, a company to develop implantable brain–computer interfaces (BCIs), enabling computers to respond to our thoughts. At the same time, entrepreneur Bryan Johnson invested $100m in online neuroscience startup Kernel, keen to give everyone a brain chip to improve mental function. Meanwhile, Facebook is working on ways to share 'full sensory and emotional experiences' with founder Mark Zuckerberg hoping to facilitate 'sharing thoughts'. When we talk with computers we convey around a measly 40 bits of information per second. Through BCIs, posthumans will up that by many orders of magnitude. Neuralink has already licensed an animal testing laboratory in California to study its ideas and technology on lab mice. Any devices to be implanted in human brains will be tested on other primates in the first instance; knowing the thoughts of these animals may have the side effect of ending such testing and granting animal rights (see page 196).

# Conscious brain-to-brain communication

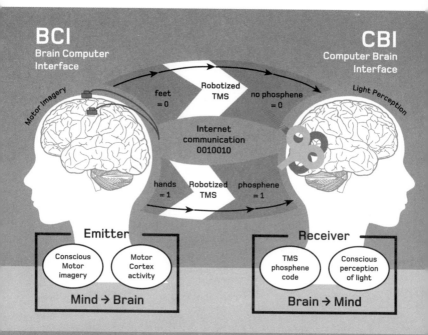

The sender on the left controls an EEG-based BCI by thinking about moving a hand or foot. The receiver on the right interprets the signal as the presence or absence of light generated by transcranial magnetic stimulation (TMS).

# Superpowers

The fictional Six Million Dollar Man had two bionic legs, one arm giving super strength and a bionic eye for zooming in. These superpowers, and more, will be available to posthumans. Telescopic contact lenses have been developed to zoom at will, but once subretinal sensors become superior to human vision these will be implanted and tuned also to see wavelengths beyond the visible. Harvard professor Federico Capasso engineered a miniature metalens 'bionic eye' in 2018 that, if scaled up, would be far superior to natural eyes. The development of soft robotic exoskeletons are underway, to help stroke victims. The tougher Guardian XO from Sarcos Robotics is also in the pipeline, allowing workers to triple what they can lift. As with previous developments, the next step will be to incorporate such strength internally. Posthumans hope to abolish pain, a technique currently in its infancy through spinal cord stimulators. They may also come equipped with a repository of different drugs built-in, enabling posthumans to speed up or slow down their metabolisms, and increase cognitive abilities.

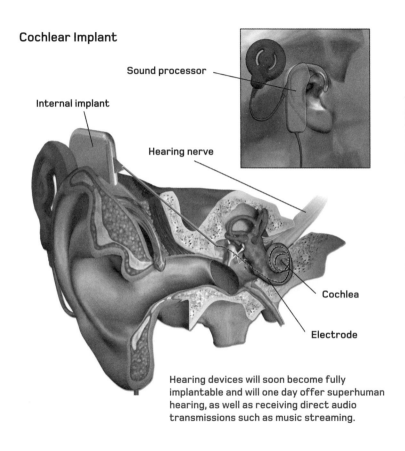

## Cochlear Implant

Sound processor

Internal implant

Hearing nerve

Cochlea

Electrode

Hearing devices will soon become fully implantable and will one day offer superhuman hearing, as well as receiving direct audio transmissions such as music streaming.

# Virtual humans

Once brain uploading becomes a reality, it will create a new posthuman era, detailed by American polymath Robin Hanson in his book *The Age of Em*. Ems (emulated humans) will become more numerous than organic humans, trillions living and working – on subsistence wages – in dense 'cities' that will appear harshly functional to us, but will be places of staggering virtual reality (VR) beauty to their inhabitants. Ems reproduce by making exact copies with the same memories and skills. If a single em is the world's best electrical engineer, it can be copied millions of times to produce a highly skilled workforce with no training required. Especially disruptive about Hanson's em society is the speed at which it runs. In 24 hours of objective time, some ems running at very fast clock speeds will work for years, measured in their time, so will be incredibly productive. Ems will live for as long as their civilization lasts, but in retirement will likely be forced to run at slower speeds – as powerless to impact the future as the organic humans living in the world outside.

Virtual cityscape

# Clans and spurs

Most VR humans of Robin Hanson's em society will be descended from a thousand diverse and qualified people scanned earlier. Future copies – and copies of copies of each person – will form 'clans'. At creation, ems are identical to others, sharing past memories and experiences before diverging slowly, implying great trust between clan members. The best few clans will dominate labour markets – Hanson suggests based on a dozen or so of the original humans. Clans would also be responsible if one member transgresses the law. Individual ems working on low wages will struggle to afford time off. To mitigate against this, they may produce 'spurs' – copies created to perform a specific task, but then terminated. This seems brutal, but spurs know a form of them will continue. If there are a hundred spurs working on a task, they may even draw lots to see which of them survives. To make up for their lack of recreational time, spurs might start out with memories of a stupendous vacation, so their truncated life doesn't appear so bad.

# Mind crime

Mind crime is the deception, torture or even involuntary termination of digital beings. Once posthumans become virtual, their effective status will be like brains in a vat – everything their senses perceive comes through artificially generated signals into their virtual brain. But if your world is entirely simulated, how do you know what to trust? Are these really your colleagues, or is this an elaborate industrial espionage simulation by your enemies to steal your secrets? What if an enemy claims to have captured your mind state and threatens to torture a million copies of you unless you do their bidding? Virtual humans are likely to go to extraordinary lengths to protect their 'mind states' to prevent them being stolen and/or copied. A future superintelligence might create internal simulations including conscious virtual beings, perhaps to predict consequences of its own actions. If these sentient virtual beings are then killed this appears to be another form of mind crime. If we are, in fact, living in a computer simulation, is anything bad that happens to us also a mind crime?

# Implications for the world economy

In a 2017 report, consultancy firm PWC predicted the world economy will have doubled in size by 2042, using gross domestic product as a measure. Once brain uploading becomes routine, American economist Robin Hanson predicts this 25-year period will be reduced to two weeks, a change far more transformative than resulted from the Industrial Revolution. In a single year this would make the economy 67 million times larger. The speed at which virtual humans will operate is critical – once brains are uploaded, it's the processor's clock speed rather than Earth's rotation that dictates time passing. To achieve the same level of growth using the physical world would take 650 years assuming the PWC figures. While physical humans (and virtual humans running on slow processors) will witness the most astonishing changes in the world around them, far beyond their control, the virtual humans running on fast processors will see life as business as usual, with change and future shock much more manageable. But in one of our years these posthumans will live the equivalent of centuries or millennia.

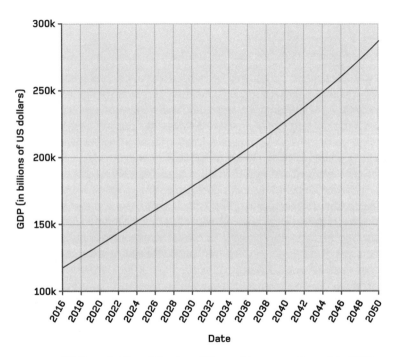

PWC's projection of the size of the world economy through to 2050.

# Does humanity have a future?

The fossil record reveals five mass extinctions, each ending the reign of Earth's dominant species. Those who study 'existential risk' argue that humans must meet the same fate if we remain an earthbound society. There have always been natural risks, but in 1945 in the New Mexico desert, the Trinity atomic test ushered in a new era. Manhattan Project scientists considered the possibility of the test igniting the atmosphere, but tested the bomb anyway . . . and got lucky, discovering that atmospheric ignition was impossible. Oxford philosopher Toby Ord christens the subsequent era as 'The Precipice' – we have created the technological means for our destruction, but not yet the accompanying apparatus to prevent it happening. The non-negligible risk of extinction we face from AI, nuclear weapons and synthetic biology (estimated at around 20% per century) is thousands of times greater than the natural threats faced previously, and is unsustainable – we must pass beyond The Precipice in no more than two or three centuries if we are to survive. Otherwise, our extinction would mean trillions of worthwhile human lives that never come to pass.

# Asteroid impacts

Sixty-six million years ago an asteroid measuring 12km (7.5 miles) across smashed into Chicxulub on Mexico's Yucatán peninsula. It is commonly thought that the event wiped out non-avian dinosaurs. While the immediate fireball, shockwave and tsunami devastated life within hundreds of kilometres, planetary-wide extinction was due to the small sulfur particles lifted from the seabed into the stratosphere. They circled the Earth, blocking out the Sun to bring on decades of extreme cooling. Three-quarters of all species perished. A large asteroid could strike Earth again and without countermeasures humanity may not survive. The risks are low but the consequences high. Recognizing this, the Spaceguard program, run by NASA and funded by the United States, catalogues all near-Earth objects, plotting their paths to see which may become a danger. Currently we appear safe and if humans become more familiar with working in space, we would be better placed to know about an asteroid heading for Earth and more capable of deflecting it. But who's to say that future humans will not deliberately target planets with asteroids for nefarious reasons?

# Supervolcanoes

A supervolcano erupts roughly every 100,000 years, the last being Mount Toba, Indonesia, 74,000 years ago. A future candidate can be found in Yellowstone, Wyoming, with continent-level eruptions 2.1 million, 1.3 million and 630,000 years ago. The last deposited a layer of ash 3m (10ft) deep over Texas. A 2014 US Geological Survey study showed how a new super-eruption would devastate the continent, with global temperatures dropping by a measurable amount. Stanford geologist Gerta Keller believes it was such an eruption in the Deccan Traps – and not the asteroid impact at Chicxulub (see page 302) – that wiped out non-avian dinosaurs. The eruption buried part of India under kilometres of flood basalt, releasing vast amounts of sulfur aerosols into the stratosphere. As in the Chicxulub impact theory, global cooling is the primary mechanism. While eruptions are difficult to predict, methods will improve and scientists are seeking ways to prevent them being so catastrophic. A 2017 NASA study looked at drilling into giant magma chambers to relieve pressure. Cooling the magma is another alternative, perhaps extracting geothermal energy from it.

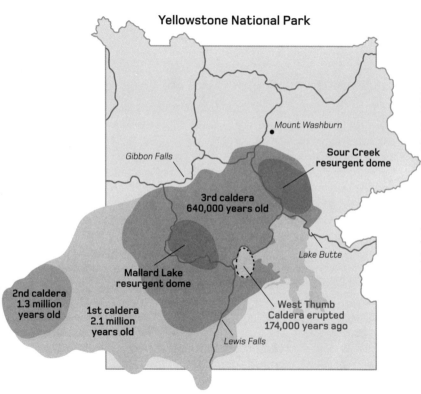

# Yellowstone National Park

Mount Washburn

Gibbon Falls

**Sour Creek resurgent dome**

**3rd caldera 640,000 years old**

Lake Butte

**Mallard Lake resurgent dome**

**2nd caldera 1.3 million years old**

**1st caldera 2.1 million years old**

West Thumb Caldera erupted 174,000 years ago

Lewis Falls

Geologists are unsure when the next Yellowstone super-eruption will occur, but expect several decades' warning.

# Nuclear annihilation

In 1945, atomic bombs destroyed the Japanese cities of Hiroshima and Nagasaki. The United States went on to test the vastly more powerful hydrogen bomb. Despite several near misses, humanity has not seen such weapons used in anger again. Development has proved hard; well into the 21st century there are only a dozen or so nuclear states. Up to now, the Non-Proliferation Treaty and the doctrine of Mutually Assured Destruction have kept the peace. While terrible, future regional nuclear conflicts do not threaten humanity's existence if contained. There are sufficient warheads to blanket the globe with devastating destructive power, but in the event of a global power war it is likely most would target enemy states. This means the immediate damage and much of the radiation 'fallout' would be restricted to the northern hemisphere. Investigations of the 'nuclear winter' theory shaped our ideas of dinosaur extinction and, in a nuclear war, burning cities would loft aerosols into the stratosphere creating a dramatic global cooling effect. Whether we'd survive depends on the length of cooling and amount of advance preparation.

# Pandemics

The Black Death is thought to have killed 75–200 million people, up to 60% of all humans, between 1347 and 1351. It took two centuries for the population to recover. More recently the Spanish flu pandemic of 1918 infected around half a billion (over one-quarter of the global population) killing 20–50 million. In 2005 Jeffery Taubenberger of the US Armed Forces Institute of Pathology announced his team had reconstructed the, by now extinct, Spanish flu virus using small DNA fragments found within victims buried in permafrost. The genome was published; in the lab it demonstrated its deadly effects on mice. After debate about cross-species transmission of bird flu, in 2011 Dutch and American scientists controversially published work showing how to make that happen. Some argue this knowledge will aid future cures; others protest that scientists are effectively providing terrorists or governments with manuals to recreate deadly diseases. How civilization has recovered from past pandemics suggests they should be considered as global catastrophes but not at the level that will threaten humanity's future.

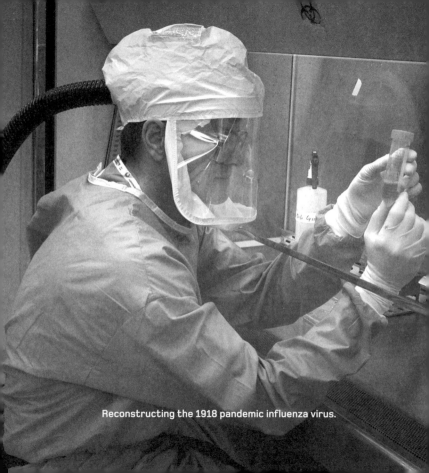

Reconstructing the 1918 pandemic influenza virus.

# Synthetic biology

Synthetic biology is the construction of new biological entities. There is rich promise of a new biologically driven industrial revolution with organic factories building new drug-delivery systems or more efficient biofuels, but a lack of regulation concerns many. An off-the-shelf library of genetic building blocks is being created, in part through international contests, allowing anyone to devise new organisms with predefined properties. This presents an anthropogenic existential risk in that we may be the architects of our own downfall. In contrast to developing nuclear weapons, synthetic biology can be, and is, practised by individuals in garages. A warning from the US National Academy of Sciences states, 'Just a few individuals with specialized skills and access to a laboratory could inexpensively and easily produce a panoply of lethal biological weapons that might seriously threaten the US population.' An obvious future application is bioterrorism, perhaps adapting deadly natural viruses, so it makes sense to accelerate technologies that might counter future risks, such as how to design, test, build and distribute medical countermeasures.

The iGEM GeoBrick, awarded at an annual global student contest to create new synthetic biology building blocks for an ever-growing library.

# Evolution of humanity

Emerging 200,000 to 300,000 years ago, in evolutionary terms *Homo sapiens* is a young species. If we survive, at what point do we cease to be human? The consensus is that, to survive long into the future, humans will have to merge with their technology and evolve into life forms we would call artificial. If future earthbound humans use nanobots to restore their bodies, external differences will be less noticeable compared with present-day humans. However, for those spending their entire lives in a microgravity environment, such as on an orbital space station, it would be much more useful to genetically engineer them to have two pairs of arms instead of both arms and legs. Those born and raised on a Martian or lunar colony will likely be taller with weaker bones, again due to the change in gravity. Virtual humans living inside computer servers will be a collection of ones and zeroes. The lives of our ancestors seem very strange to us, but even hunter-gatherer communities created art. Our virtual descendants will be stranger still, but will likely still make art and study science.

# The simulation hypothesis

Are you living in a computer simulation? Swedish philosopher Nick Bostrom's answer is that one of the following statements is true: humans will likely become extinct before reaching a posthuman state; the fraction of posthuman civilizations interested in running ancestor simulations is extremely small; we are almost certainly living in a computer simulation. Relatively soon we'll have the power to create simulated worlds populated by vast numbers of virtual humans. According to Bostrom's first statement, the Universe is real, but we'll be extinct before then. The second statement assumes that posthumans could run simulations, but won't want to. If simulations are run, however, we're likely living in one – given the many trillion humans who'd inhabit them versus the few billion on Earth now. What if we inhabit a 'resource-constrained' simulation, one in which the programmers have trouble paying the electricity bill? We wouldn't want the Universe turned off, but the potential value of the future would be less than that in a rich, physical Universe, making extinction less of a tragedy.

We could be living in a simulation programmed by
other advanced human or other beings.

# The Singularity

Humans have been the undisputed most intelligent species on Earth for at least the last 40,000 years, but not for much longer. In a 1993 essay, computer scientist Vernor Vinge christened 'The Singularity', the beginning of the posthuman era when we shall have created machines smarter than ourselves. American futurist Ray Kurzweil popularized the term in his 2005 book, *The Singularity is Near*, describing it as when a single machine intelligence matches the thinking power of all humans. Filmmaker James Barat titled his book on the subject, *Our Final Invention*. Science, technology and even art will outstrip anything humans can imagine today. Whether we benefit will depend on the goals the machines have before they surpass us. We are only the dominant species because, collectively, we are smarter than our competition; once our own creations can outthink us, they may work with us, ignore us or remove us because we obstruct their goals – our fate will rest in their hands. Kurzweil expects The Singularity to occur as early as 2045; 90% of experts predict it will have happened by 2075.

# Ray Kurzweil's Countdown to Singularity

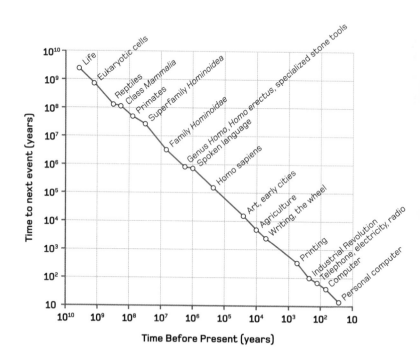

# Utility functions

A utility function makes artificial intelligence (AI) 'happy', providing a numerical score to optimize the task being performed. It motivates the AI by assigning a value to each possible future world the AI's actions will create. For an autonomous car, for example, there's great value in any journey that avoids hitting a pedestrian, ensuring this outcome is achieved whenever possible. Transitioning from AI to artificial general intelligence (AGI), the AGI's values will likely be encoded in a utility function making the choice of this extremely important – given how our own values change over time. In calculations based on utility functions, there are rational bets a machine might make that a human would not and this is especially the case when the machine is looking forward to the vast potential of the future Universe. A one-off opportunity offering access to all the resources of our galaxy with a 5% chance of success, versus a 95% likelihood of destroying Earth and all its inhabitants, might be considered a gamble worth taking, regardless of what any humans might think.

# A model-based, utility-based agent

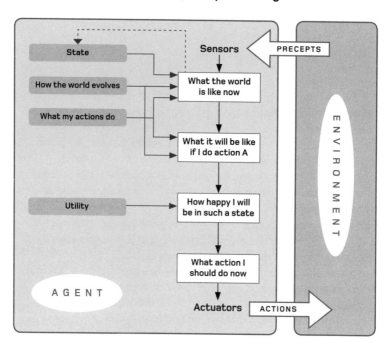

Simulating an action to see how it would alter an AGI's utility function informs its decision on whether to act.

# Pathways to AGI

In 2016, Deep Mind's AlphaGo defeated world Go champion Lee Sedol, a feat not expected until the mid-2020s. Deep Mind co-founder Demis Hassabis says its mission is to 'solve intelligence'.

Once AI is part of our lives, we often cease to think of it as AI; for example, face detection in a camera or a character's behaviour in a videogame. It now seems a simple problem to make machines understand our speech and answer back, all down to a breakthrough in neural network technology in 2012. Experts give a 90% probability of reaching human-level general intelligence before the end of the 21st century. Brain emulation is one route, while machine-learning algorithms using huge amounts of data are another. In 2018, OpenAI taught a robotic arm to manipulate delicate objects in its fingers, training the software on a simulated version of the arm running on very fast computers so it experienced the equivalent of a century in real time. Should this approach be translatable to more general applications, AGI might arrive sooner than the experts expect.

Shadow Dexterous robot hand holding a lightbulb.

# Intelligence explosions

Physically, there is relatively little difference between the brains of mice, dolphins, chimpanzees and the brightest of humans. Yet even if machines initially only exceed human-level intelligence by a little, many thinkers believe there is nothing to prevent them altering their own designs to quickly go far beyond. Swedish philosopher Nick Bostrom terms this an 'intelligence explosion'. AGI might be the intended goal, but once the machines are smarter than the humans who designed them, by recursive self-improvement they are better equipped to continually make themselves smarter still.

There is no obvious physical limit on intelligence. While human brains are restricted to what fits within our skulls (with neural signals travelling along pedestrian biological wiring), machine brains could be the size of planets, information criss-crossing unfathomable neural structures at the speed of light. Unless the control problem (see page 324) has already been solved, humans will likely have become extinct long before this point.

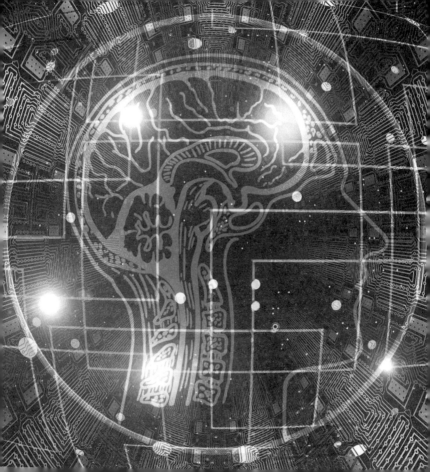

# The control problem

Once machines are significantly smarter than humans, the game is up and the future out of our hands. If wanting beneficial outcomes for humans, we must solve the 'control problem' before superintelligence is achieved. Ideally this means instilling goals into the machine to promote humanity's long-term interests, but could also involve mechanisms to limit the superintelligence's capabilities once it becomes super smart. But limiting a superintelligence's abilities restricts its usefulness. We could specify rules, such as Isaac Asimov's Laws of Robotics. An alternative suggested by Nick Bostrom in his book *Superintelligence* (2014) is 'indirect normativity' in which we give the AI a process to arrive at the rules or values it is to pursue – it might be that we're not the best people to think what tasks an AI should be set, so instead we ask it to 'achieve that which we would have wished the AI to achieve if we had thought about the matter long and hard'. This has the added benefit of allowing for future changes in our values. We should specifically accelerate research on the control problem rather than on the wider field of AI.

Asimov's first law of robotics states that a machine must always act in such a way that prevents a human coming to harm. This becomes more pertinent as we approach a new age in which machines increasingly take control.

# Perverse instantiations

In *Superintelligence*, Nick Bostrom shows how solutions to the control problem can fail by specifying imprecise goals without anticipating the consequences. Suppose we want humanity to be happy. We might instruct the superintelligence to 'make us smile'. While learning, the machine intelligence could do its best to please us, but it may come to think its utility function is better rewarded by paralysing our facial muscles in a permanent grin. In another example, Bostrom considers an AI tasked with control of a factory manufacturing paperclips – the AI converts the Earth and then the observable Universe into paperclips in a scenario known as 'resource profusion'. Limiting the manufacture to, say, one million paperclips doesn't help. However many times they are counted, the machine can never be certain (in Bayesian probability terms) that it's counted out exactly a million, so must devise ever more elaborate means of checking, perhaps by turning all the matter in the solar system into a powerful computer to analyse the problem – again resulting in resource profusion. As we approach this future we must be careful what we wish for.

# Supermachines

If there's a high ceiling to intelligence, then the potential rewards of creating a superintelligence are huge, especially if there's a similarly high limit on new technologies that can be invented. Combining the two, supermachines can be created on astronomical scales. They need not be for peaceful purposes. If one country creates superintelligence to wage war on another, it could achieve a decisive military advantage – at least in the short term – by creating such engines of destruction that it's akin to one side fighting with spears while the other attacks with advanced fighter jets. But what if the machines turn on their creators? It seems most efficient for superintelligence to optimize its environment by controlling nature at a fundamental level. Instead of creating vast single-purpose supermachines, by manipulating atoms it could use swarms of nanobots to transform atoms from one configuration into another – say, changing an aeroplane into a paperclip factory. Humans are made of atoms; our value to the superintelligence must be greater than the sum of our parts.

The Bagger 288, the world's biggest mining machine, will be dwarfed by supermachines of the future.

# Conscious machines

Some definitions of The Singularity explain it as the moment that a machine intelligence becomes self-aware. Philosophers have long debated what it means to be conscious. Distinguished thinkers such as John Searle and Sir Roger Penrose don't believe it's possible for machines to become conscious and so do not believe superintelligence can be created. However, the AGIs discussed in this book do not require consciousness to function. We know intelligence that leads to consciousness has been created at least once (in humans) and, even though the origins are uncertain, most scientists recognize consciousness in other animals, such as the octopus, which has a very different neural structure extending through its tentacles. If the future intelligences we create do become self-aware, given they're not even biological entities, we would predict their consciousness to be very different from the human version. Even today's AIs 'think' in strange ways, sometimes completing video games with very novel strategies. Devising a scientific theory of consciousness may even be a task for a future superintelligence.

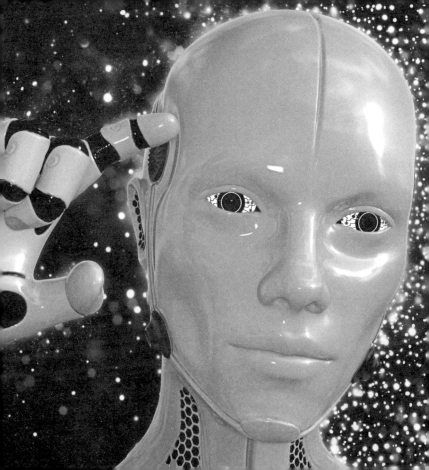

# Our cosmic endowment

There are many risks to the future of humanity, but if they can be overcome and if we can create superintelligence that is beneficial for humans, quite possibly merging with it, then the rewards are astronomical. 'Resource acquisition' is an instrumental goal of any superintelligence, meaning we have reason to believe the superintelligence will desire to spread through the Universe – as well as more prosaic reasons to think it will be capable of doing so. Yet there is no evidence of other superintelligences already there. This suggests the potential space we can expand into is very large and may only be limited by the portions of the observable Universe we can still impact.

These considerable resources – a cosmic endowment – in the observable Universe could provide future humans with the equivalent share of a galaxy each. The future may be far richer and more wondrous than we can possibly comprehend – one reason it is the essential task of our time to ensure we cherish and safeguard its huge potential.

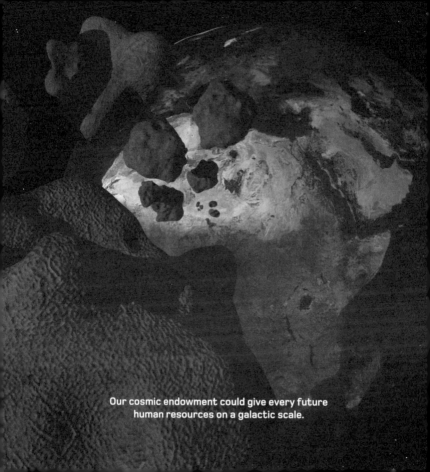

Our cosmic endowment could give every future
human resources on a galactic scale.

# Space travel and colonization

From Orville and Wilbur Wright travelling 36.5m (120 ft) at Kitty Hawk in 1903, through Charles Lindbergh's 1927 Atlantic crossing, to Neil Armstrong and Buzz Aldrin setting foot on the Moon 384,000km (239,000 miles) away in 1969, powered flight has made astonishing strides. Since Gene Cernan closed Apollo 17's lunar module hatch in 1972, we have regressed and the furthest we now send humans is just a thousandth of that distance to where the International Space Station (ISS) hangs in low Earth orbit.

A future that includes human spaceflight is not inevitable. Space travel is expensive and dangerous; much of the money to be made there is also likely to be spent there. If we don't become spacefaring, however, our extinction is inevitable. Whether asteroid impact, supervolcano, nuclear war or simply the Sun swallowing Earth, there will be future events we cannot outrun. Many moral philosophers believe the greatest good can be achieved by maximizing our potential across the whole Universe, making the colonization of outer space the key moral imperative of our time.

# Commercial spaceflight

Until recently only nation states were able to launch satellites, then people, into space. The Russians began with Sputnik in 1957 and then, four years later, Yuri Gagarin aboard Vostok One. Then NASA took men to the Moon 'for all mankind'; it's the American flag that flies in six locations on the lunar surface. Times are changing. Resupplying the ISS since 2012, it is the commercial operation SpaceX that has led the way in spaceflight.

For humanity to become truly spacefaring, it's likely profit will be a driver. SpaceX and Boeing have lucrative commercial crew contracts to give the United States its own (if private) astronaut launch capability. Going commercial means driving down the astronomical costs of escaping Earth's 'gravity well'. Current revenues come from launching satellites, but other opportunities such as asteroid mining (see page 340) will follow soon. The UN Outer Space Treaty forbids nation states claiming new territory beyond Earth, but will not prevent profit from driving corporations to boldly go into the solar system and exploit its resources.

An artist's impression of the SpaceX Crew Dragon docking with the International Space Station during a mission for NASA's Commercial Crew Program.

# Reusable rockets

Imagine stepping onto an Airbus in London, flying to New York, then parachuting out over Manhattan while the aircraft is deliberately ditched in the Atlantic. This was the approach initially taken to spaceflight. The Shuttle was the first to have some reusability, but even then individual launches still cost $450m. For commercial companies to become involved that number needed slashing; Blue Origin's New Shepard made the first successful powered landing from space in 2015, while SpaceX has pioneered landing from low Earth orbit with their Falcon 9. Large-capacity conventional rockets cost over $160m per launch. To build a roughly equivalent Falcon 9 costs around $40m, but to fuel it costs only $250k. Only paying for the fuel when reusing the rocket is why this is so disruptive to the space launch industry. SpaceX's Falcon Heavy and Starship rockets are also reused. NASA's Space Launch System is not – it's so expensive that only two launches a year will be possible. In contrast, SpaceX rockets and Blue Origin's New Glenn will land and re-fly in as little 24 hours – revolutionizing costs.

A double landing of first-stage cores from SpaceX's Falcon Heavy.

# Asteroid mining

A new space race is beginning, led by space-mining companies such as Planetary Resources – backed by the Luxembourg government, which sees investment in space as securing a prosperous future. The prize isn't just the trillions of dollars' worth of high-grade precious metals available in near-Earth asteroids – it's building a new space-based society during the second half of the 21st century. Every kilogram lifted into space is expensive; given all the same raw materials exist throughout the solar system, travellers should collect what they need as they go. First will be water. Estimates suggest there's as much water on nearby spacerocks as in the North American Great Lakes. Since rocket fuel is just hydrogen and oxygen, orbital processing plants will be able to use this water to refuel satellites and spacestations by the 2030s. The mined materials will remain off-world, where they will be used to underpin orbital construction projects such as space habitats or solar shields to lower global temperatures. Later this century, resources in the main asteroid belt between Mars and Jupiter will help humans begin to colonize the outer solar system.

An artist's impression of NASA's OSIRIS-REx spacecraft
preparing to take a sample from asteroid Bennu.

# Space tourism

In 2001, Dennis Tito paid a reported $20m to spend eight days on the ISS, becoming the world's first space tourist. Others soon followed, and when Scaled Composites won the Ansari X Prize for completing two suborbital flights in 2004, a new era in space tourism beckoned. Richard Branson bought the company, creating Virgin Galactic, and the first successful test flight to the edge of space took place in 2018. When NASA ends its ISS support the plan is for private enterprise to turn it into a space hotel. Houston's Axiom is already taking reservations ($55m each) for its bespoke Philippe Starck designed habitation module to host 16 tourists and be added to the ISS. But the future lies further afield. Humans never enjoying the wonders of the solar system is like no one visiting the Grand Canyon. One day we'll float above Saturn's rings and strap on wings to fly like birds through its moon Titan's thick atmosphere. Humans will scale the ice mountains of Pluto, visit cloud cities above Venus, explore Europa's ocean and travel to the summit of Mars' giant volcano, Olympus Mons.

A NASA poster advertising space travel, rendered in a retro style.

# Moonbase

The 1960s space race benefited from having a nearby target. In the future, the fact that the Moon can be reached within three days means that technologies for living off-Earth will be trialled there. Mars Society President Robert Zubrin's 'Moon Direct' proposal outlines a low-cost, five-year plan for achieving this by 2025; NASA instead proposes a Lunar Gateway space station for then, with a Moonbase waiting until the 2030s.

Both lunar poles have sufficient water for manufacturing rocket fuel, while iron, aluminium, silicon and titanium can all be mined. Early moonbases will likely be 'printed' by autonomous robots using lunar regolith, before larger self-sustaining cities are built within lava tubes. A massive radio observatory, shielded from the interference generated on Earth, is proposed for the far side of the Moon; other areas will become home to spaceship factories and fuel depots. Space tourists will visit the original Apollo landing sites while elderly residents of luxurious retirement homes enjoy both the low gravity and the glorious blue-marble views overhead.

An artist's conception of a lunar base

# Mars colonization

**W**ill humans make permanent homes on the red planet? Dutch project Mars One wants to emulate early human colonists who left their homes knowing they'd never return.

SpaceX plans to have one million people living on Mars by the end of the 21st century, to form a sustainable colony. The $250k journey is not officially a one-way ticket, however, as the spacecraft need to return for later colonists. Each Starship will hold 100 settlers (plus cargo) and many such rockets will leave together every 26-month launch window. Much will be created by robots sent ahead. NASA is also developing small, lightweight, nuclear fission reactors to power settlements, since planet-wide dust storms preclude reliable solar power. Water is plentiful at both poles but also in mid-latitudes, where huge glaciers lie covered by only thin layers of rock. The lack of atmosphere means living within sealed environments, whether lava tubes or other structures that protect from cosmic rays, but the 24.6-hour day will help future Martians adapt.

Colonizing Mars: an artist's conception of the early stages of establishing a colony on the red planet.

# Terraforming

Terraforming attempts to transform other worlds into something Earthlike. Two obvious candidates are our nearest neighbours, the rocky planets Venus and Mars. On the inner edge of the 'habitable zone', Venus is almost the same size as Earth, but a runaway greenhouse effect has made it the hottest solar system planet. A dense layer of sulfuric acid clouds conceals the fact that it has 243-day 'day', so if humans want a regular biological clock it would have to be created entirely artificially. Mars, towards the outer edge of the habitable zone, is more promising. A sustainable colony has better long-term prospects if human Martians can breathe Martian air. This requires making the atmosphere 140 times thicker and creating the appropriate composition. Gravity is one-third of Earth's, but the day is almost the same length and its axial tilt similar, giving defined seasons. We know Mars was once warm and wet and rather Earthlike and the goal is to return it to that state; proposed methods are to detonate massive nuclear explosions at the polar caps to release $CO_2$ and to bombard the planet with asteroids to supply other atmospheric gases.

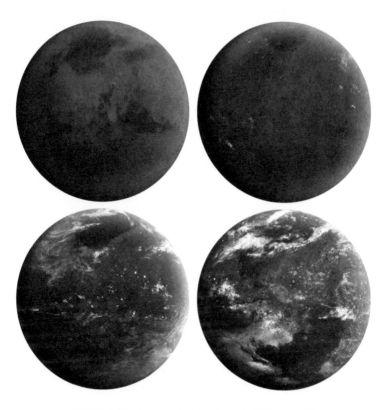

A series of images created to show what Mars might
look like at various stages while being terraformed.

# Solar system travel

SpaceX's Starship interplanetary transport system uses methane and liquid oxygen fuel because both can be generated anywhere in the solar system, including the plains of Mars, the moons of the outer planets or even the distant Kuiper Belt. Such chemical rockets refuelling in Earth orbit could reach Mars in four months, while a trip to Saturn would take around three years. Technological innovation is needed for future humans to fill the solar system. The first step is likely to be solar electric propulsion, currently being developed by NASA's Game Changing Development Program. Solar sails, giant thin films propelled by radiation pressure from powerful lasers, are another option. Further ahead, rockets will be powered by fusion power, once that has been perfected (see pages 164–7). Scale is important. It will always be expensive to send handfuls of astronauts anywhere. One reason for the leap in scale, such as with the Starship, with its capacity for 100 travellers, is that this leads to lower ticket prices when the cost is divided by the many hundreds travelling.

An artist's conception of a solar electric propulsion system.
Solar electric propulsion requires a fraction of the fuel of chemical
rockets and allows continual acceleration throughout the voyage.

# Space elevators

Advanced civilizations will need more efficient methods than chemical rockets to transport objects from planetary surfaces into space. Visionary author Arthur C. Clarke popularized the space elevator in his novel *The Fountains of Paradise*. Such an elevator's cable must reach geostationary orbit 36,000km (22,000 miles) above Earth's equator, but would reduce the cost of sending things to space by two orders of magnitude. Hence, this is an active research area across global institutions. Japanese Obayashi Corporation proposes beginning construction in 2050, but not even carbon nanotubes or graphene ribbons are strong enough to revolutionize Earth-to-space transport in this way. We could build space elevators above the Moon and Mars with their lower gravity, so these will likely become testing grounds, furthering off-Earth economic development. Once one elevator has been built, others will become far cheaper, leading to the creation of a megastructure orbiting a planet, the cables like spokes in a giant wheel. Later, variants may appear such as a direct 'elevator' between Pluto and its tidally locked moon, Charon.

This illustration by artist Pat Rawlings shows the concept of a space elevator as viewed from the geostationary transfer station looking down the length of the elevator towards Earth.

# Viewing exoplanets

The first exoplanet – one that orbits a star other than our Sun – was only discovered in 1995. The Kepler Space Telescope showed that planetary systems are the norm across our galaxy and astronomers have now targeted exoplanets for the 2021 James Webb Space Telescope to observe. This has a mirror so large it will be able to perform transit spectroscopy on the atmospheres of nearby alien worlds, analysing their constituents.

Detailed telescopic images of exoplanets remain decades away. However, the Breakthrough Starshot programme proposes sending physical probes to the Alpha Centauri planetary system, just over four light years away, which would arrive in the coming decades. This entails travelling at a significant proportion of the speed of light, which can be achieved using miniaturization. A succession of sensors built into tiny chips will be propelled using solar sails, speeding them to survey, for the first time, a planetary system beyond our own, perhaps even finding liquid water on a planet's surface, or evidence of life itself.

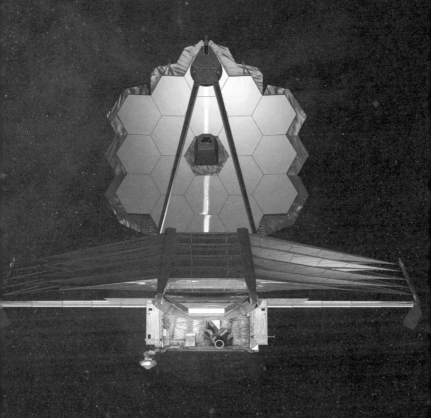
An artist's impression of NASA's James Webb Space Telescope.

# Orbitals and ringworlds

In the 1970s American physicist Gerard O'Neill devised detailed plans for future human orbitals in space, proposing that the raw materials should come from the Moon or mined asteroids. Using solar power, O'Neill colonies (built from two counter-rotating cylinders to avoid gyroscopic effects and maintain fixed rotation) would provide controlled gravity for efficient industrial production and beautiful stepped terraces, parks, rivers and lakes for an agreeable living environment. At 20km (12.5 miles) long and 8km (5 miles) across, they would also have an outer agricultural ring to support farming.

Why terraform over long timescales when humans can build these large, pleasant, self-sustaining living environments in the future, aided by robot space-assemblers? In Iain M. Banks's utopian Culture novels, most advanced races live this way. Sci-fi author Larry Niven's *Ringworld* (set in 2850) takes the concept further, portraying an artificial doughnut-shaped habitat with a surface area equivalent to around three million Earths, orbiting its parent star.

Exterior view of a ringworld
space colony that was part of a
NASA Ames study in the 1970s.
Artistic rendering by Don Davis.

# Worldships

The first human voyages to the stars will take thousands of years. Depending on life-extension treatments, those setting off may not be the ones who arrive. The best proposal we have to enable a space-based society to survive over such a timescale is the 1984 'wet worldship' of British rocket engineers Alan Bond and Tony Martin. Much of its 250km (155 mile) length would be taken up with 8,633 billion tonnes of fuel and resources, the remaining 2,021 billion tonnes being an ocean habitat section. Such generational spaceships would require extraordinarily reliable systems. They could become interstellar arks, preserving humanity while exploring the Universe, but is it moral to consign future generations to an isolated life in interstellar space? Also, future would-be generational colonists have a dilemma: should you embark on a long early worldship voyage or are you better off waiting a century, by which time new technology may become available that reduces the transit time to a mere fifty years? Descendants of the original early crew might reach their destination to discover a thriving human colony already in place.

The work of the The British Interplanetary Society, this depiction of the
Bond/Martin 'wet worldship' shows it mining the gas giant planets for fuel.

# Von Neumann probes

Computer pioneer John von Neumann created the mathematics used to model the spread of civilization through the Milky Way, via a concept christened a von Neumann probe. From the originating solar system this would reach a nearby star system where it would go on to build two or more new probes that would then travel to further star systems, where each would do the same. Our galaxy is around 100,000 light years across, but even travelling at conservative speeds (perhaps 10% of the speed of light) the probes would reach every star system within one to five million years. What is often misunderstood is that the abstract mathematics involved applies equally well to would-be human colonists, for instance those aboard a worldship. After one thousand years travelling to Tau Ceti, humans could arrive and create a new human civilization, building more worldships to continue the exploratory drive beyond. In this way, human civilization might spread across the entire Milky Way in as little as a million years, beginning from some point in the 2100s when the technology should be available.

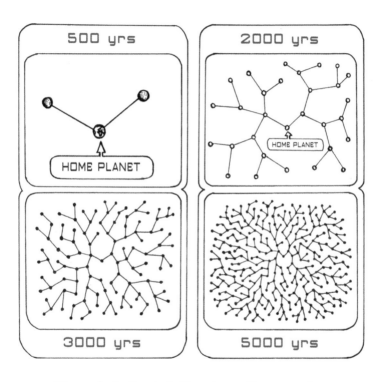

Stages of galactic colonization using von Neumann probes.

# The Fermi paradox

At lunch at Los Alamos in 1950, physicist Enrico Fermi asked, 'Where is everybody?' The subtext was, 'Where are the aliens?' The same laws of nature that apply on Earth (teeming with life) are meant to apply throughout the cosmos, yet everything we observe in space is explained by inert processes. Von Neumann probes make things even more perplexing. Earth is a relatively young planet – if extraterrestrial life is prevalent, we'd expect our galaxy to have been colonized thousands of times over. Yet it seems extraterrestrial intelligence is rare. Some argue we're the very first, but this view is uncommon. It's likely that should humans expand into the galaxy over the next tens of thousands of years, we will encounter aliens. This 'first contact' could be one of the most significant moments in future history, provided we recognize what is happening. One commonly held belief is that any spacefaring aliens will be machine intelligences, long since evolved from their organic progenitors. Aliens might be so very alien, we may not recognize intelligent life when staring us in the face.

# Alcubierre drive

When Einstein proposed special relativity in 1905, the speed of light seemed an apparently unbreakable cosmic speed limit. Approaching it, you become ever more massive (infinitely so at light speed), your length in the direction of travel shrinks (to zero at light speed), and time passes increasingly slowly. This time dilation means future spacefarers travelling within a whisker of the speed of light could traverse the Milky Way within an existing human lifetime, despite our galaxy being 100,000 light years across. However, friends and family left behind would see the journey take over 100,000 years. If you could travel faster than light, some observers would see you arrive at your destination before you left your starting point. That didn't stop relativity theorist Miguel Alcubierre proposing a 'warp drive' to the British Interplanetary Society in 1994, which would make it possible to modify space—time to allow a spaceship to travel faster than light. Since then, other scientists have refined the idea, including reducing the energy demands, making such a device more of a practical possibility for the far future.

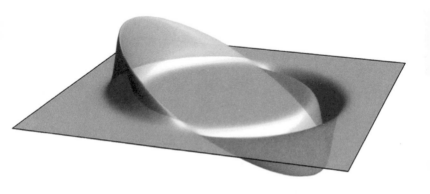

Instead of travelling faster than light the Alcubierre drive would enable advanced humans to move a bubble of space–time faster than light while remaining inside it.

# Very advanced technologies

In his book *Profiles of the Future*, Arthur C. Clarke claimed, 'Any sufficiently advanced technology is indistinguishable from magic'. To visitors from the Middle Ages, planes criss-crossing the skies, with humans venturing to other worlds, would be unfathomable wizardry. Even today's world, in which smart devices control smart homes and access to the world's knowledge is just a command away, would seem fantastic to visitors from 1990.

Before he died, Sir Isaac Newton remarked, 'I seem to have been only like a boy playing on the sea-shore and diverting myself in now and then finding a smoother pebble or a prettier shell than ordinary, whilst the great ocean of truth lay all undiscovered before me.' Over nearly three centuries since, we have waded a little further out and found the water to our liking. By the end of the 21st century, physicist Michio Kaku predicts, 'We will have the power of gods'. Partnered by superintelligent machines, we may become invisible at will, move objects with our thoughts and even rebuild the Universe atom by atom as we follow Newton's example.

Arthur C. Clarke

# De-extinction

Steven Spielberg's *Jurassic Park* introduced de-extinction to the world, using dinosaur DNA from amber-preserved, cretaceous-era mosquito blood to recreate creatures gone for 65 million years. Now controversial organization Revive and Restore is promoting the concept with more recently extinct creatures. In 2016, Beth Shapiro, author of *How to Clone a Mammoth*, announced the dodo genome had been sequenced. Discussions are underway with Mauritius conservation experts and politicians about bringing the bird back after three centuries. Harvard geneticist George Church heads a team that's sequenced much mammoth DNA. He believes he'll create a hybrid mammoth/elephant embryo by 2020, but doesn't think it ethical to implant that into another living creature. Given we protect endangered species, it seems a natural next step to de-extinct animals we've lived alongside. But these creatures died out because their ecosystems could no longer support them. Is it fair to bring them back to live in captivity? We don't yet need to face these questions for dinosaurs, but going through the 21st century we may have to.

# Room-temperature superconductors

**D**utch physicist Heike Kamerlingh Onnes discovered
superconductivity in 1911. Placing solid mercury into liquid
helium just four degrees above absolute zero, all electrical
resistance disappeared. The finding wasn't especially useful
given the ultralow temperature (−269°C/−452°F). Then, in 1986,
Georg Bednorz and Alex Müller discovered 'high-temperature
superconductivity' in advanced ceramics, up to −135°C (−211°F)
– important because these could be cooled using readily available
liquid nitrogen, so enabling powerful superconducting magnets
such as those used in MRI scanners. For superconductivity to
impact everyday future life, it needs another step change, moving
to room temperatures. Electric currents can flow for years
through superconducting wires with no measurable degradation,
so superconducting transmission lines would have no power
loss between generating source and consumer, dramatically
reducing energy needs. This also makes room-temperature
superconductors perfect batteries, electric current endlessly
flowing in superconducting storage facilities until required.

Superconductors expel internal magnetic fields, allowing trains or cars to levitate above tracks with air resistance the only source of drag.

# Nanotechnology and radical abundance

In 1986 American engineer Eric Drexler published *Engines of Creation: The Coming Era of Nanotechnology*. In the work, he proposed atomically precise manufacturing systems based on nanoscale machines that could build things by guiding the placement of reactive molecules. The things these machines built would include more manufacturing systems (self-replication).

In the aftermath of Drexler's book, the term 'nanotechnology' became fashionable and appropriated to mean any work at the nanoscale. In 2013, Drexler revisited his vision of 'radical abundance'. Within a few decades he predicts high-throughput, atomic-scale manufacturing will be able to produce vast quantities of most products people might want, at low cost. Radical abundance would overturn the global economy, enabling the poorest in society to have access to more than the wealthiest today. With heavy industry a thing of the past, the environment could be restored. The disruption of 3D printing provides a foretaste of what will come.

An atomically precise nanoscale planetary gear mechanism in which the spheres represent atoms of different types.

# Invisibility

Our longing to be able to become invisible may happen. Possible methods include: becoming completely transparent; bending light around something so we see what's behind it; or projecting what is behind an object to in front of it. Visible light is only a small portion of the electromagnetic spectrum, which goes from radio waves at one end to gamma rays at the other. Radar 'sees' via radio waves, but 'stealth' tries to make objects invisible to radar by either absorbing signals or reflecting them away from the receiver. First seen in the F117 stealth fighter, the technology's routine in ships and tanks. Metamaterials, with unusual repeating composite structures, force light to take unusual paths around an object to achieve invisibility. This is easier with microwaves because the wavelength of the radiation matches that of the structure – Sir John Pendry's spherical cloak was demonstrated with microwaves in 2008. Theoretically this would work in visible light – but only once materials with the necessary properties have been invented.

A material with internal irregularities scatters an incoming beam of light in all directions (top). The disc, made from metamaterials, is visible, scattering the wave from the left. Illuminated from above using a specific pattern, the disc becomes invisible as the wave passes through it undisturbed (bottom).

# Antigravity

**G**ravity is unusual, so weak that a handheld magnet can cause an object to defeat the entire gravitational pull of the Earth and leap into the air and, unlike electromagnetism and the nuclear forces that govern matter, it apparently lacks an anti-force. We can simulate the absence of gravity by flying parabolic arcs (as in NASA's 'vomit comet') and recreate its presence by rotation to induce centrifugal forces. If we can generate the effects of gravity in this way, future humans may also be able to remove gravity's effects, turning it on (for instance during long-duration space journeys) or off (for example with flying cars). In 1998, three astronomers discovered that, at very large distances, the expansion of the Universe was accelerating, entirely contrary to expectations. Scientists call the force that repels distant matter dark energy – it's the closest thing we know to antigravity. Whether or not dark energy is the key to creating antigravity technology, the revolution in physics it promises will help us progress dramtically. To get there, we may need assistance from the superintelligences we create.

Trainee astronauts aboard NASA's KC–135 aircraft, affectionately known as the 'vomit comet'.

# Telekinesis

Telekinesis, moving something with the power of your mind, was long thought wizardry but is becoming commonplace; anyone can command a drone with the help of a simple skull cap. The secret is an electroencephalogram-based brain–computer interface (BCI). In Europe alone, 300,000 people suffer from spinal-cord injury. The Brain–Machine Interface Lab at the Ecole Polytechnique Fédérale de Lausanne (EPFL), Switzerland, has pioneered BCIs for wheelchairs and exoskeletons, partially freeing the severely disabled from being dependent on caregivers.

With technology increasingly embedded in everything through the Internet of things, thought control will inevitably become widespread, albeit via a device or implant and not through innate telekinetic power. However, once brain uploading becomes successful, humans living in virtual environments will by definition have mental control of anything. Possessing such godlike telekinetic powers in the physical Universe may one day be possible with a deeper understanding of matter, energy and space–time.

An assistant in the laboratory at EPFL in Switzerland is
transported by a wheelchair that he is controlling only with his mind.

# Teleportation

In 2017, Chinese scientists led by Pan Jianwei broke the world record for teleportation, extending it to 1,400km (870 miles) from Earth to an orbiting satellite. Disappointingly for *Star Trek* fans this refers to quantum teleportation, the transmission of the exact state of an atom or photon. IBM's Charles Bennett devised the theory of quantum teleportation in 1993, but so far the largest objects to which it has been applied are rubidium atoms. The philosophical meaning of physical human teleportation is unclear. If it's disassembling Captain Kirk's molecules and physically transmitting them to another location before reassembly, then he is surely killed in the process. If it's only scanning Kirk and sending the information to another location for construction from the blueprint, using new matter, then what happens to the original? Also, Bennett's teleportation relies on the phenomenon of quantum entanglement, which appears infeasible on macroscopic scales. However, in the virtual Universe of brain uploading (see page 276) ems will be able to teleport, and their mind states will be accustomed to living with duplicates of themselves.

# Time travel

In theory we can actually see the future for ourselves. We normally move forward at the rate of one second per second, but it's possible to change that. Since Einstein proposed special relativity explaining the links between space and time, we've known by travelling close to light speed we can go arbitrarily far into the future, whether that's a day, a year or even a million years. Just three days travelling at the same speeds we generate in particle accelerators, the crew of a rocket would find themselves in the year 2100. General relativity promises a further time boost by grazing a black hole and some will likely use both techniques to explore even further into the future. There is a catch. If you didn't like the future you saw, we don't think you could come home. Mathematical physicist Stephen Hawking proposed the 'chronology protection conjecture' that dictates we can only travel forwards in time, never back. Breaking the conjecture would allow you to violate causality, perhaps as you try to alter the future you saw but disliked.

Travelling to another galaxy through
a hypothetical wormhole would also
send you backwards in time.

# The fate of Earth and of the Universe

Making predictions about the future is fraught with problems, but once we look far enough ahead we find our feet back on firmer ground – at least for the next few billion years. The physical laws that govern the Universe point to inevitable consequences, even if our current limited understanding of time or dark energy leaves some questions open, and the possibility of future understanding being radically different. In only a few thousand years on our island Earth, in an apparently unremarkable corner of the galaxy let alone the Universe, humans have come to understand so much of what governs everything. It has been remarkable progress. We have made great strides in understanding how the Universe began and how, if nothing happens to intervene, it might end. If the evolutionary descendants of humanity survive into these distant epochs, with the same desire to understand physical laws and exercise control over the Universe, then even this farthest future can be shaped to our will. Long after the stars have gone out there remains potential for worthwhile lives to be lived.

# Longer days

About 4.4 billion years ago a Mars-sized planetoid called Theia smashed into the early Earth, sending a portion of the mantles of both bodies into orbit. Within a century the debris coalesced into the Moon, just 20,000–30,000km (12,500–18,500 miles) away. Back then the length of a day on Earth was around six hours, but the new Moon created huge tides that swept across Earth's surface. Tidal forces have been slowing Earth's rotation ever since – when the dinosaurs were wiped out a day was 20 minutes shorter than now. In about 180 million years, a day will be 25 hours long.

The Moon's been moving away from Earth ever since it was formed. Although the rate at which the Moon is receding is slowing, meaning it will never break free from Earth's orbit, 50 billion years from now Earth and Moon will become tidally locked, both bodies permanently presenting the same face to each other in a 45-day rotation period, unless the Sun becoming a red giant (see page 392) prevents this happening.

# The new Pangaea

Earth is shaped by plate tectonics; the Himalayas began rising when the Indian plate rammed into the Eurasian plate 50 million years ago, and are still growing. Until 180 million years ago all Earth's landmasses were locked in a single supercontinent called Pangaea, which split into Laurasia to the north and Gondwanaland to the south, before further breakups and mergers formed the jigsaw puzzle of today's continents.

NASA's Lageos satellites measure continental drift at a pace slower than the growth of a human fingernail. Africa and Europe are colliding. The Alps and Pyrenees will grow to Himalayan heights and, within 50 million years, the Mediterranean will have closed. Perhaps a little before then, the East African Rift Valley will have widened until parts of Somalia and Ethiopia break away to form a large island in the Indian Ocean. Beyond this, though harder to predict, the expectation is the eventual formation of a new supercontinent labelled Pangaea Proxima, with all Earth's land joined once again, around 250 million years from now.

**A rough appoximation of Pangea Proxima**

# Earth becomes uninhabitable

The Sun is a stable star, but over the course of its middle age it is warming up. Every billion years it becomes 10% more luminous and this means what's called the 'habitable' or 'Goldilocks' zone of the solar system, where liquid water can exist, is shifting further out. Estimates differ on the exact timescale, but between 500 million and a billion years from now Earth's oceans will evaporate. If preserving water on Earth is important to life at that point, solutions will exist. One would be to give the planet a solar shield like a giant parasol in space, preventing some of the Sun's radiation reaching the surface.

A grander scheme might be to move Earth into an orbit further out. Yale astronomer Greg Laughlin has proposed a mechanism an advanced civilization might use to do this, adding 30% more energy to Earth's orbit by sending it half as far away again from the Sun using objects from the outer solar system as gravity tugs. It would take roughly a million asteroid fly-bys, but could maintain Earth's biosphere for a few more billion years.

# Swallowed by the Sun

Since forming 4.6 billion years ago, the Sun has been a stable main sequence star (see page 399). This has allowed astronomers Klaus-Peter Schröder and Robert Connon Smith to forecast its future. Both luminosity and temperature will increase 1% every 110 million years, peaking in 2.55 billion years' time. From then on it will gradually cool while still brightening, until 5.4 billion years from now, when its diameter will be 37% bigger than today. Once the Sun's core hydrogen fuel is spent, things change more quickly as the Sun turns from a stable star to a red giant. Looking 7.4 billion years ahead, over a short period of only 5 million years, the Sun, burning helium, will engulf Mercury and Venus in quick succession as it expands. It will lose mass, reducing its gravity and suggesting Earth's orbit might widen, but this is not so. Increased tidal forces and dynamic drag will mean the Earth–Moon system is also engulfed. For an advanced civilization to avoid this fate, the minimum safe distance would be to manoeuvre Earth at least 15% further out than it is today leaving Earth to orbit the white dwarf star the Sun becomes.

# Universal expansion

A merican astrophysicist Ethan Siegel says with every second, 20,000 faraway stars pass beyond the reach of any potential future human civilization. American Edwin Hubble observed that the further away from us an astronomical object is, the greater the speed it is receding from Earth. Space itself is expanding, so every point in the Universe is receding from every other, ignoring 'local' motion. Through the second half of the 20th century, the presumption was the big bang 13.8 billion years ago had begun this expansion – the question was if there was sufficient mass in the Universe to halt it. Unexpectedly, in 1998 astronomers discovered that at very large distances the rate of expansion was increasing through a new force labelled 'dark energy'. The volume of space humanity can impact is our 'Hubble sphere' – beyond this the Universe recedes faster than the speed of light, making access impossible. The boundary of our Hubble sphere currently lies 15 billion light years away, but the observable Universe has a radius of 46 billion light years. This means only 3% of all galaxies in the observable Universe are available to future humans.

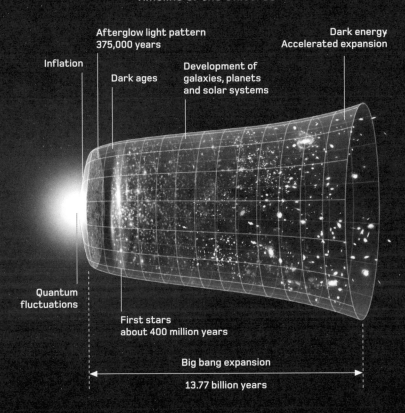

# Timeline of the Universe

Afterglow light pattern
375,000 years

Dark energy
Accelerated expansion

Inflation

Dark ages

Development of
galaxies, planets
and solar systems

Quantum
fluctuations

First stars
about 400 million years

Big bang expansion

13.77 billion years

# The local group

The Andromeda Galaxy and our own Milky Way dominate the 'Local Group', our intergalactic neighbourhood. The Triangulum Galaxy is the next biggest and a host of smaller galaxies orbit the big two. Andromeda is 2.5 million light years away, so when we view it we're looking 2.5 million years into the past. In 2012, astronomers Roeland van der Marel and Sangmo Tony Sohn calculated that it's heading our way and in four billion years will collide with the Milky Way. There's a lot of space between stars, so direct collisions are unlikely. Some stars will be expelled from both galaxies and the Sun will likely shift outward from its current location, 26,000 light years from the galactic core, to as much as 160,000 light years out. In 100 billion years, a merger of all the galaxies in the local group will be underway that will last up until a trillion years in the future. Two trillion years hence, this super galaxy will have become the only area of the Universe we can observe and unless humanity becomes an intergalactic species long before that, this will be the only galaxy left we can affect.

The Andromeda Galaxy

# The Universe goes dark

At 13.8 billion years, the Universe sounds rather old, but it may have a quintillion (a billion billion) years to go. *The Five Ages of the Universe* by Fred Adams and Greg Laughlin describes the future evolution of the cosmos and places us early in the Stelliferous Era, notable because of the light of stars. For most of the future, the Universe will be dark. The brighter a star, the sooner it dies. Proxima Centauri, the nearest star to our Sun, is a red dwarf so faint it's invisible to the naked eye. More than three-quarters of the stars in the Universe are red dwarves and they will burn for 10 trillion years. Somewhere between 100 and 1,000 trillion years from now supplies of interstellar gas will have been exhausted meaning stars cease forming. The Degenerate Era that follows will see the Universe dominated by red dwarves, white dwarves (fading stellar cores), black holes and neutron stars. Even after red dwarves have spent their fuel, Oxford's Anders Sandberg suggests advanced future civilizations will be able to merge dead stars to reignite stellar cores for some time, should starlight be important to them.

# The Longevity of Stars

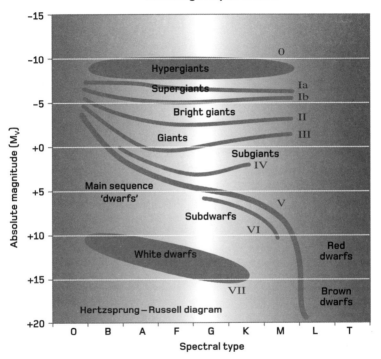

Hertzsprung–Russell diagram

The brightest stars (towards the top of the diagram) burn their fuel and are extinguished much more quickly than those at the bottom. As they age, main sequence stars move from top left towards bottom right.

# Heat death

The second law of thermodynamics states that entropy, the measure of disorder, tends to increase in an isolated system over time. It was William Thomson, later to become Lord Kelvin, who first applied this on a universal scale in the 1850s and coined the term 'heat death'. The Degenerate Era, once star formation has ended ($10^{15}$ years from now), is thought by many to be an effective end to the future, but far-futurist Anders Sandberg believes this is when the Universe becomes interesting. His aestivation hypothesis suggests a reason we don't see intelligent extraterrestrials might be because they're hibernating for the next few trillion years, until colder future temperatures enable massive improvements in the efficiency of overall computation. If the most important consideration is maximizing the value of the future, waiting until then to act instead of using up resources now will enable advanced civilizations to do more. After around $10^{40}$ years the Degenerate Era transitions to the Black Hole Era. These, the only objects remaining, slowly evaporate via Hawking radiation. By $10^{100}$ years only low-energy electrons and positrons remain in a very Dark Era.

William Thomson,
Baron Kelvin

# The big rip

Forecasts of the stars going out and heat death rely on calm projections of the Universe's evolution. Dark energy has thrown that into doubt. When we talk about distant objects in the Universe receding from us, it's actually the space–time between that is expanding. With dark energy accelerating that expansion, a new possibility was revealed by American theoretical physicist Robert Caldwell in 2003. Should dark energy grow stronger, he suggested a 'big rip' may tear everything apart, right down to the very fabric of space–time. The original lower bound for such an event was 22 billion years, but in 2016 Diego Sáez-Gómez reduced this to just 2.8 billion years from now.

If the big rip occurs, our descendants will have front row seats. Sixty million years before it happens, the Milky Way will be torn apart. Three months before the end of the Universe even the solar system will disintegrate. Earth explodes with half an hour to go and humans are small enough to observe everything until the final millisecond.

# Big rip countdown

**$10^{-19}$ seconds to go:**
Atoms destroyed

**30 minutes to go:**
Earth explodes

**3 months to go:**
Solar system disintegrates

**60 million years to go:**
Milky Way torn apart

**22 billion years before the big rip**

The
**BIG
RIP**

TODAY

# The big crunch

The idea of a big crunch, in which the Universe stops expanding and begins to shrink and eventually collapse into itself, has been around nearly as long as the earliest proposal of the big bang. Even with the discovery of dark energy it remains a possibility – there are models of gravity in which the effects of dark energy could be reversed, with Stanford's Andrei Linde calculating that this could happen within 10 to 20 billion years. Linde doesn't necessarily believe the future will unfold this way. We can find out over coming decades, using very precise astronomical observations to determine the density of dark energy at different times in the past to infer our future. If the big crunch lies in wait, humanity doesn't have long in which to maximize the value of the Universe – we would already be halfway through. This makes the potential future small in cosmological terms, and our existence less important. That's unless the big crunch leads to a 'big bounce' with the Universe oscillating and beginning again, and the descendants of humanity finding a way to survive the transition.

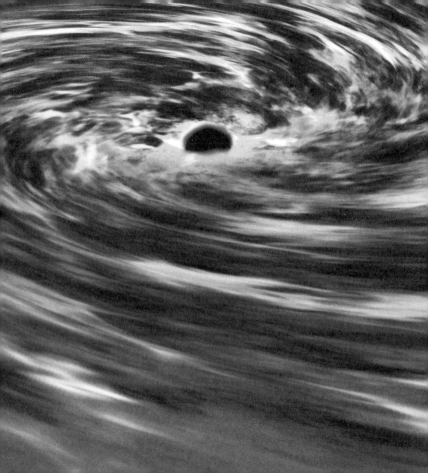

# Cycles of time

A different beginning and end to the Universe was proposed by theoretical physicist Roger Penrose in his 2010 book *Cycles of Time*. The second law of thermodynamics has entropy increasing over time, so the Universe becomes less ordered. Winding the clock back implies the most highly ordered state in all time was at the big bang. Yet most theories presume the Universe's initial conditions were 'random' or 'chaotic' – the very opposite of some special state. To overcome this inconvenient truth, Penrose proposes the Universe takes a neverending journey through different 'aeons', in which the high-entropy state at the end of one aeon becomes the low-entropy state to begin the next – which can only happen if there's a transformation in scale between the two. His theory of conformal cyclic cosmology implies previous aeons on smaller scales. Penrose predicts we should see echoes of these in the cosmic microwave background (CMB) radiation, where colliding supermassive black holes will produce circular patterns. Detections have been claimed, but the jury's out as to whether our furthest future is just the beginning of a new aeon or Universe.

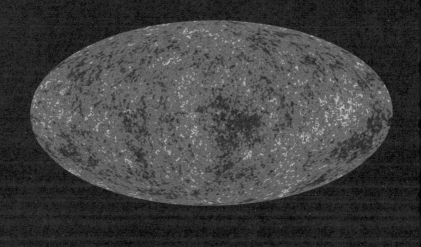

As our map of the cosmic wave background becomes more
precise, scientists will look for new patterns that might indicate
previous aeons of the Universe.

# Glossary

### Android
A robot having human appearance.

### Artificial general intelligence (AGI)
Machine intelligence that is capable across a broad spectrum of abilities, as opposed to narrow artificial intelligence that is only expert in a particular field, such as playing chess.

### Asilomar principles
The 2017 Asilomar AI principles are a template for creating beneficial artificial intelligence in the future. They resulted from a conference at Asilomar State Beach, California.

### Biodiversity
The variety of plant and animal life in a particular habitat or the whole world. A high degree of biodiversity is considered desirable for the welfare of humans and Earth.

### Bit (computing)
A unit of information that takes a value of 0 or 1 in binary notation.

### Black box
A system whose internal workings are hidden, so the reasons for specific outputs, given the inputs, are not apparent.

### Butterfly effect
The idea that a minuscule change in the initial conditions of a dynamic system can completely alter how it evolves over time.

### Byte (computing)
The smallest unit of memory in many computer systems, normally consisting of eight bits.

### Deep fake
An artificial-intelligence-based technique for creating fake images, audio or video of real people to depict events that never occurred.

### Disruption
Disruptive innovation is a transformational change, creating a market where none existed previously or an unanticipated technology that has profound effects. Uber, Netflix and Airbnb are examples of disruptive companies, while movable type or reusable rockets are examples of disruptive technologies.

### DNA
Deoxyribonucleic acid, a self-replicating molecule that carries genetic information in a double-helix structure.

### Gig economy
A labour market characterized by freelance work or short-term contracts in which workers are paid for the specific 'gigs' that they undertake.

### Hash (blockchain)
Used as a noun or verb, a hash is a mathematical function that converts information into an alphanumeric string 64 characters long. Hashing creates this string.

### High-level language (computing)
A means of constructing a computer program that has a high level of abstraction when compared with machine code (the instructions that are executed by a computer's CPU or central processing unit). Many forms are written using elements of natural language. Examples are Fortran, Haskell, Prolog, Java, Python and C++.

### Holocene
The geological epoch that began around 11,650 years ago with the end of the last glacial period. Some propose it has now been superseded by a new epoch named the Anthropocene.

### International Space Station (ISS)
Constructed between 1998 and 2011, the ISS is a permanently occupied multinational facility in low-Earth orbit that is expected to operate until at least 2030.

### Light cone
A term used in both special and general relativity to indicate the path of a light beam emanating from a specific event in space–time, travelling in all directions. Helping define causality, only events on or

within a past light cone are able to influence the specific event; similarly it can only influence future events on, or within, its own future light cone.

## Main sequence (star)
The Hertzsprung–Russell diagram is the plot of star colour versus brightness; most stars fall within a continuous band on this diagram, which is classified as the main sequence phase of stellar evolution.

## Megacity
A city having more than ten million inhabitants.

## Merkle tree (blockchain)
The structure of the blockchain, defining how the hash values within blocks is stored and how the chain is linked together, as a means for efficient data verification (devised by Ralph Merkle).

## Monte Carlo simulation
A method of repeated random sampling used in Bayesian statistics. By simulating an event a large number of times (using a computer model), the probability of different outcomes can be inferred.

## MOOC
A massively open online course delivered from a university and made available, normally without charge, to an unlimited number of potential students. Common platforms are Coursera, Udacity and edX.

## Nuclear winter
The severe, prolonged cooling effect caused in the aftermath of a nuclear conflict in which widespread fires lead to the transportation of soot particles into the stratosphere where they will remain for decades, blocking direct sunlight.

## OpenAI
An influential artificial intelligence research organization founded in 2015 'to advance digital intelligence in the way that is most likely to benefit humanity as a whole' by promoting safe and beneficial AI and disseminating tools as widely as possible.

## Order of magnitude
An approximate measure of the size of something, described using powers of ten. If one quantity is two orders of magnitude larger than another, it will be roughly one hundred times bigger.

## Planetary gearing
A gear system in which one or more outer (planet) gears revolve around a single central (Sun) gear, taking its name from early use to drive models of the solar system.

## Post-gender
The idea that in the future the concept of binary gender will be eroded and eventually disappear through gender becoming fluid and ultimately irrelevant – culturally and biologically.

## Probability distribution
Individual events (such as tossing a coin) are considered to be random samples taken from a probability distribution that specifies that the sampling outcome will fall within a certain range. A coin toss has two possible outcomes so is governed by the binomial distribution. Other commonly used distributions are the normal, Poisson and gamma.

## Renewables
A natural energy source that is not depleted with use, such as wind, wave or solar power. Whether energy from biomass such as wood burning should be considered renewable is considered controversial.

## Seastead
A floating permanent habitat in international waters and not under the jurisdiction of any nation.

## Stellar mass
An astronomical unit of mass to describe objects in comparison with the Sun (about $10^{30}$kg) For example the bright star Vega is 2.135 stellar masses.

## Sustainability
Not depleting natural resources, allowing an ecological balance to be maintained.

# Speculative timeline

**2025** Majority of freight vehicles are autonomous

**2029** The SpaceX Starship Heart of Gold lands the first humans on Mars

**2030** The UN's 17 Sustainable Development goals come to fruition

**2030** China becomes the world's richest nation

**2033** The first ice-free Arctic summer

**2034** Continuous human presence on the Moon is established

**2037** A rudimentary dog translator is released onto the market

**2038** First in-orbit rocket-fuel factory created, thanks to asteroid mining

**2040** A universal basic income is implemented across the West

**2048** First human baby brought to term in an artificial womb

**2050** Human–robot marriage is legalized

**2060** The PROTO Tokamak generates electricity commercially through nuclear fusion

**2085** First space probes reach the Alpha Centauri system

**2100** Construction begins on an Earth-based space elevator

**2115** First human to live to age 150

**2125** World government is formed

**2145** Martian terraforming begins

**2170** First human brain uploaded

**2185** Mars colony declares independence

**2250** The first worldship launches for the star Tau Ceti

**2075** The Singularity makes the future beyond it unknown

**2400 years** Humans make first contact with extraterrestrials

**2500 years** Posthumans build a Dyson swarm around the Sun

**3000 years** All life on Earth has been paradise-engineered into one of many degrees of bliss

**296,000 years** The Voyager 2 space probe makes its closest approach (4.7 light years) to the star Sirius

**50 million years** The Mediterranean Sea is closed as Africa merges with Europe

**180 million years** Day becomes 25 hours

**250 million years** Earth's landmasses come together to form a new supercontinent

**600 million years** The Moon has moved too far from Earth for total solar eclipses to occur

**750 million years** Earth's oceans evaporate

**4 billion years** Andromeda Galaxy collides with Milky Way

**7.4 billion years** Sun becomes a red giant star engulfing Earth

**100 billion years** Local group of galaxies begins to merge

**1 trillion years** Local group of galaxies is the only matter remaining within the observable Universe

**500 trillion years** Star formation ends

**550 trillion years** The Universe goes dark

**$10^{40}$ years** Black holes are the only significant objects remaining in the Universe

**$10^{100}$ years** Black holes have evaporated leaving only low-energy electrons and positrons

**$10^{150}$ years** A new aeon of the Universe begins

**3 billion years** The Universe ends in the big rip, ending time

**15 billion years** The Universe ends in the big crunch, ending time

# Index

# Picture credits

First published in Great Britain in 2019 by

Quercus Editions Ltd
Carmelite House
50 Victoria Embankment
London EC4Y 0DZ

An Hachette UK company

Copyright © Quercus Editions Ltd 2019
Text by Keith Mansfield

Edited by Anna Southgate
Designed by Dave Jones
Proofreader: Richard Beatty
Indexer: Patricia Hymans

PB ISBN 9781787477278
EBOOK ISBN 9781787477261

Printed and bound in China